PIONEER CRAFTS FOR KIDS

- •40 Craft Projects for Children

- •10 Craft Projects for Youth

- •20 Reproducible Bible
  Memory Verse Coloring Posters

- •6 Reproducible Student
  Awards and Certificates

Compiled by Neva Hickerson

Neva Hickerson, Editor
Christy Weir, Consulting Editor
Phyllis Atchison, Assistant Editor
Patty Hambrick, Bonny Linder, Lynnette Pennings, Contributing Writers
Susan Adkins, Sheryl Haystead, Contributing Editors
Carolyn Gillmon, Designer
Chizuko Yasuda, Illustrator

Library of Congress Cataloging in Publication Data applied for.

ISBN 0-8307-1423-5

CONTENTS

MAKING THE MOST OF PIONEER CRAFTS FOR KIDS

Taking risks, venturing beyond the boundaries, moving toward a goal no matter what the cost. That was the spirit of the folks called pioneers, who left their homes and ventured west toward a better life. Traveling west meant long, dusty rides in covered wagons, encounters with adversity and seeing the unspoiled beauty of God's creation. Today we can read about these adventures in published journals kept by pioneers as they traveled.

Settling down to a "better life" included lots of hard work and cooperation and "making do" with whatever resources were available. There were barn-raisings and quilting bees, homesteading, harvesting and hoedowns.

We hope you and your students enjoy learning about pioneer life as you complete the projects in *Pioneer Crafts for Kids*. And as you do, maybe you'll discover a bit of the pioneer spirit in yourselves!

CHOOSING CRAFTS FOR YOUR CLASS

Pioneer Crafts for Kids is a resource for teachers and parents—a book full of ideas from which you will choose craft projects for your child or class. We've chosen projects that relate to pioneer life, are age-level appropriate and fun. But we haven't done *all* the work for you!

Your job is to know the students you'll be working with. Consider their interests and skills. Also, consider your class size and the amount of class time you will devote to each day's craft. Then, select crafts you think your students will enjoy and be able to complete in the allotted time. Don't feel confined to the crafts in a particular age-level section. You may want to adapt a craft from a younger or older age level.

In addition, you will want to consider what materials you have on hand, what materials are available in your area and what materials you can afford to purchase. Don't feel confined by the materials listed for crafts. In some cases you will be able to substitute materials in order to use something you already have.

We encourage you to see *Pioneer Crafts for Kids* as the foundation of your craft program. Then, see yourself, the teacher or craft director, as an essential element in planning enjoyable and successful craft projects for children and youth.

LET THEM BE CREATIVE!

In this fast-paced age of information and pressure to perform, arts and crafts may be one of the few times when a child is allowed to express the unique person God has made him or her to be. In arts and crafts a child may say, "I think an orange and purple flower would look nice," or "I want my cabin to have windows on all sides." Imagine how much fun it is to make such decisions when most decisions are made for you each day. That is why it is important to allow children the chance to be creative when making crafts. Don't expect every child's project to turn out the same. Don't insist that children "stay in the lines."

If possible, provide a variety of materials from which children may choose. And finally, ask children about their choices and affirm them. This is a way of showing children they are loved by you and by God. Also, your affirmation will encourage children to apply creative thinking to other areas of life.

"PIONEER LIFE" SECTIONS

Every craft in this book includes a section entitled "Pioneer Life." These sections are designed to help you enhance craft times with interesting facts about pioneer life. They provide open-ended questions that will encourage creative thinking and verbal expression.

Craft time can be a refreshing time when students don't have to "get the right answer," but have an opportunity to communicate what they think and feel in an environment where individuality is encouraged.

PREPARING TO DO CRAFTS

• If you are planning to use crafts with a child at home, here are three helpful tips:

1. Focus on the projects in the section for your child's age, but don't ignore projects that are listed for older or younger ages. Elementary age children enjoy many of the projects grouped under "Crafts for Young Children" and they can do them with little or no adult assistance. And younger children are always interested in doing "big kid" things. Just plan on working along with the child, helping with tasks the child cannot handle alone.

2. Start with projects which call for materials you have around the house. Make a list of items you do not have which are needed for projects you think your child will enjoy. Plan to gather those supplies in one expedition.

3. If certain materials seem too difficult to obtain, a little thought can usually lead to appropriate substitutions. And often the homemade version ends up being a real improvement over the original plan.

• If you are planning to lead a group of children in doing craft projects, keep these hints in mind:

1. Choose projects which will allow children to work with a variety of materials.

2. Make your selection of all projects far enough in advance to allow time to gather all needed supplies in one coordinated effort. Many projects use some of the same items.

3. Make up a sample of each project to be sure the directions are fully understood and potential problems can be avoided. You may find you will want to adapt some projects to simplify procedures or vary the materials required.

4. Many items can be acquired as donations from people or businesses if you plan ahead and make your needs known. Many churches distribute lists of materials needed to their congregation and community and are able to provide crafts at little or no cost. Some items can be brought by the children themselves.

5. In making your supplies list, distinguish between items which every individual child will need and those which will be shared among a group.

6. Keep in mind that some materials may be shared among more than one age level, but only if there is good coordination among the groups. It is extremely frustrating to a teacher to expect to have scissors, only to discover another group is using them. Basic supplies which are used repeatedly in craft projects should usually be provided to every group.

HELPFUL HINTS

USING GLUE WITH YOUNG CHILDREN

Since preschoolers have difficulty using glue bottles effectively, you may want to try one of the following procedures. Purchase glue in large containers (up to one gallon size).

a. Pour small amount of glue into several shallow containers.

b. Dilute glue by mixing a little water into each container.

c. Children use paste brushes to spread glue on project.

OR

a. Pour a small amount of glue into a plastic margarine tub.

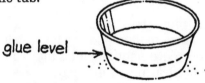

glue level →

b. Give each child a cotton swab. The child dips the cotton swab into the glue and rubs glue on project.

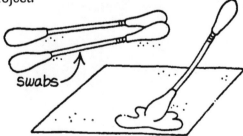

swabs

c. Excess glue can be poured back into the large container at the end of each session.

HOW TO MAKE PATTERNS

You will need: Tissue paper, lightweight cardboard, pencil, scissors.

a. Trace pattern from book onto tissue paper.

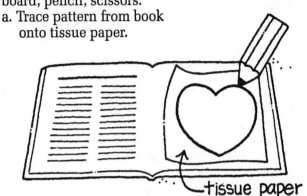

tissue paper

b. Cut out tissue paper pattern and trace onto cardboard.

c. Cut out cardboard pattern.

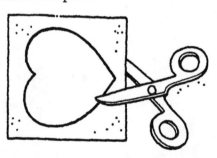

CUTTING WITH SCISSORS

When cutting with scissors is required for these crafts, take note of the fact that some of the children in your class may be left-handed. It is very difficult for a left-handed person to cut with scissors that were designed to be used with the right hand. Have available in your classroom two or three pairs of left-handed scissors. These can be obtained from a school supply center.

GROUP QUILT PROJECT

Pioneer Crafts for Kids includes five different quilt square projects (see Contents). The squares can be made into individual projects, or completed as a group project—a quilt.

The completed quilt might be hung as a decoration in a classroom or church fellowship hall, given to a needy family or a convalescing senior citizen. Also, a quilt can be sold to raise money for church group outings or a missions project.

Below are directions to make a simple quilt (for a single bed) using any of the quilt square projects described in *Pioneer Crafts for Kids.* Of course, you can modify these instructions to make a smaller or larger quilt.

Materials:
Scissors, measuring tape, 44 9-inch (22.5-cm) decorated muslin quilt squares (made from one or more of the quilt square projects in this book), 9 yards of 45-inch (112.5-cm) solid color cotton fabric for additional squares and backing, 9 yards of 7/8-inch (2.1-cm) quilt binding, yarn for tying 2 yards of 90-inch (225-cm) 100% bonded polyester batting, thread, straight pins, needle, sewing machine, iron.

Instructions:
•Preshrink all fabric.

•Cut 44 9-inch squares from solid color fabric.

•With right sides together and using a 1/2-inch (1.25-cm) seam allowance, sew a solid color square to a muslin square on one side (sketch a). Then sew a solid color square to the opposite side of the muslin square (sketch b). Continue adding squares to this row until you have a total of eight alternating squares.

•Begin the second row of squares with a muslin square and add seven alternating squares.

•Using a 1/2-inch (1.25-cm) seam allowance, sew the first row of squares to the second row (sketch c).

•Continue to make a total of 11 rows of squares. Sew additional rows together as de-scribed above to complete quilt top.

•Trim seams and press them to one side so they will lay flat.

•To make backing: Cut additional solid color fabric into two 33½x88-inch (83.75x220-cm) pieces. Using a 1/2-inch (1.25-cm) seam allowance, sew the two pieces together lengthwise (sketch d).

•Lay backing wrong side up on a flat surface. Lay batting on top of backing. Place quilt top, right side up, on top of the batting (sketch e). Batting should protrude 1 inch (2.5-cm) all the way around quilt. Pin through all three layers to hold in place.

•Thread needle. Beginning at the center of the quilt, use large basting stitches to sew to one corner. (You do not need to knot the ends of the thread.) Repeat to baste from the center to each corner (sketch f).

•Thread needle with a single strand of yarn and do not knot. At the top left corner of the quilt, where four squares intersect, make one stitch through layers of quilt. Cut yarn, leaving 2-inch (5-cm) tails. Knot yarn close to quilt top (sketch g). Repeat this process at each intersection.

•Following manufacturers directions, sew quilt binding around edges of quilt.

•Remove basting stitches.

a.
muslin square
solid color square
b.
c.

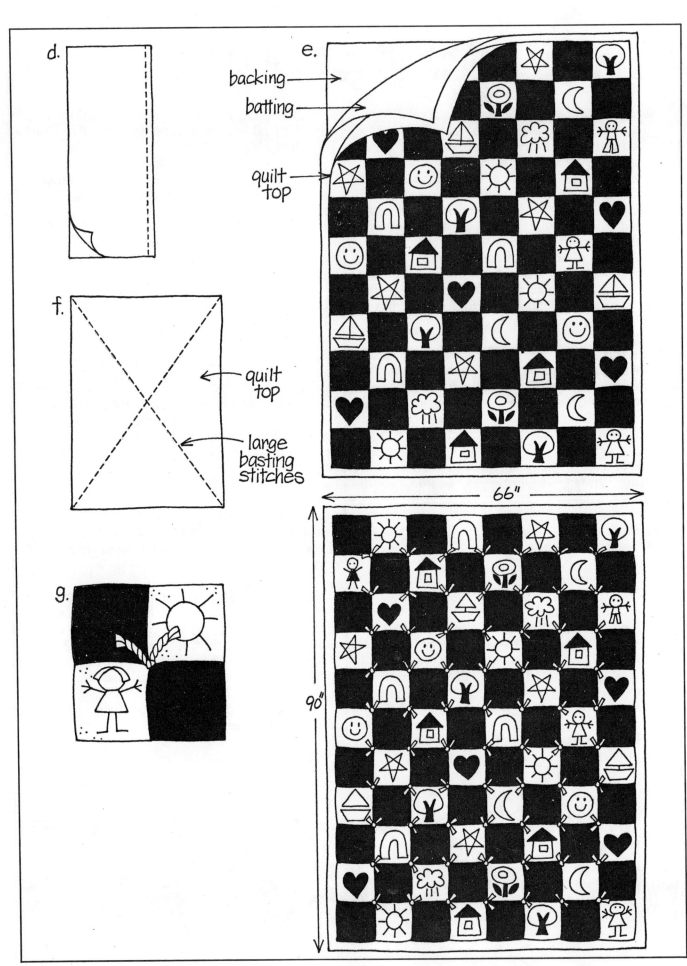

d.

f.

quilt
top

large
basting
stitches

g.

e.

backing

batting

quilt
top

66"

90"

QUILT SQUARE DESIGNS

The designs below can be used as decorating ideas for a variety of projects in this book. You may want to make a photocopy of this page for each student.

Shoofly

Log Cabin

Basket

Flying Geese

Heart

Rail Fence

STENCIL PATTERNS

These stencil patterns can be used to decorate a variety of projects in this book. To make a stencil: Trace stencil pattern onto tissue paper and cut out. Lay tissue paper pattern on cardboard or bristol board (available at art supply stores) and trace.

Use craft knife to cut out shapes, leaving outer area intact. Students lay stencil on craft project and carefully paint within cutout area. You may want to create additional stencil patterns of your own.

SECTION 1 / AGES 2-5
CRAFTS FOR YOUNG CHILDREN

Craft projects for young children are a blend of, "I wanna do it myself!" and "I need help!" Each project, because it is intended to come out looking like a recognizable something, usually requires a certain amount of adult assistance—in preparing a pattern, in doing some cutting, in preselecting magazine pictures, in using the iron, etc. The younger the child, the more the adult will need to do, but care must always be taken not to rob the child of the satisfaction of his or her own unique efforts. Neither must the adult's desire to have a nice finished project override the child's pleasure at experimenting with color and texture. Avoid the temptation to do the project for the child or to improve on the child's efforts.

Some of the crafts have enrichment and simplification ideas included with them. An enrichment idea provides a way to make the craft more challenging for the older child. A simplification idea helps the younger child complete the craft more successfully. If you find a child frustrated with some of the limitations of working on a structured craft—although most of the projects in this book allow plenty of leeway for children to be themselves—it may be a signal that child needs the opportunity to work on more creative, less structured materials: blank paper and paints, play dough, or abstract collages (gluing miscellaneous shapes or objects onto surfaces such as paper, cardboard or anything else to which glue will adhere). Remember the cardinal rule of thumb in any task a young child undertakes: the process the child goes through is more important than the finished product.

VEGETABLE STAMP QUILT SQUARE

(ONE-DAY PROJECT / 30 MINUTES)

Note: If you wish to use these squares to make a quilt, see page 7 for quilt instructions. If you do not wish to make a quilt, children can use squares as blankets for Rocking Cradle.

Materials: Muslin, various colors of fabric paint, shallow pans for paint, various firm fruits and vegetables (carrots, potatoes, celery, apples), paring knife, scissors, ruler, newspapers, iron, water, towel.

Preparation: If you will be making a quilt, wash and dry muslin to preshrink. Cut muslin into 9-inch (22.5-cm) squares—one for each child. Wash and dry fruits and vegetables. Cut into pieces suitable to be held by small hands. On flat edge of each piece, carve a simple shape to form a stamp (star, heart, triangle, square, lines, etc.) or use the shape of the vegetable itself. Cover work surface with newspapers. Pour or squeeze paint into shallow pans.

Instruct each child in the following procedures:

- Dip vegetable and fruit stamps into paint and then press onto fabric. Repeat, dipping stamp in paint for each print.
- Allow to dry for at least four hours. Then adult should iron back of quilt square to set paint.

Enrichment Idea: Allow children to decorate more than one square.

Pioneer Life: (You may want to bring in a quilt to show children.) **How do you keep warm at night? Pioneers kept warm by using blankets made from colored scraps of fabric. These warm blankets were called quilts. What colors did you choose for your quilt square?**

carrot

potatoes

celery

muslin square

fabric paint

ROCKING CRADLE

(ONE-DAY PROJECT / 30 MINUTES)

Note: The Rocking Cradle can be used with the Spoon Doll (p. 14) and the Vegetable Stamp Quilt Square Blanket (p. 12).

Materials: Brown craft paper or brown paper grocery bags, glue, craft knife with extra blades, scissors, tempera or acrylic paints in bright colors, paintbrushes, shallow containers for paint, pencil, measuring tape, newspapers. For each child—one 42 oz. oatmeal container with lid.

Preparation: Glue lids to the oatmeal containers. Cut brown paper into 9½×17-inch (23.75×42.5-cm) sheets. Glue a brown sheet of paper to each oatmeal container (sketch a). Trace lid onto brown paper and cut out—two for each cradle. Glue paper circles to top and bottom of oatmeal containers. Use craft knife to cut cradle as shown in sketch b—one for each child. Cover work surface with newspapers. Pour paint into shallow containers. Fill several containers with water.

Instruct each child in the following procedures:

- Paint a design on cradle (sketch c). Let dry.

Enrichment Idea: Have children glue paper on oatmeal containers, then cut as in sketch b. Make stencils using patterns on page 8. Children paint stencil designs on Rocking Cradle.

Pioneer Life: **What kind of bed did you sleep in when you were a baby? The pioneers made wooden cradles for their babies. The babies liked to be rocked in their cradles. Sometimes parents sang as they rocked their babies to sleep. What song will you sing as you rock your "baby" to sleep?**

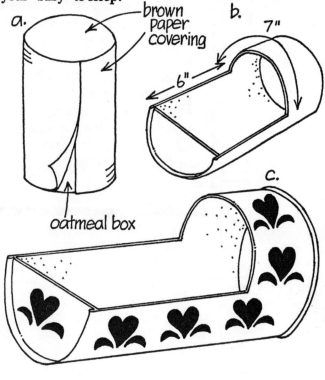

a.

brown paper covering

b.

7"

6"

oatmeal box

c.

FRINGED VEST
(ONE-DAY PROJECT / 30 MINUTES)

Materials: Construction paper in a variety of bright colors, glue, scissors, ruler, masking tape. For each child—one large paper grocery bag. Optional—paper cutter.

Preparation: Use scissors to cut grocery bags as shown in sketch a—one bag for each child. Make sure neck and arm openings are large enough to allow for freedom of movement. If there is printing on the bag, turn vest inside out. Fold masking tape around neck opening to reinforce (sketch b). Use scissors or paper cutter to cut 1- and 2-inch (2.5- and 5-cm) squares from construction paper. Cut some of the squares in half diagonally to make triangles. Cut at least 20 shapes for each child.

Instruct each child in the following procedures:
- Use scissors to cut fringe around bottom of vest (sketch b).
- Decorate vest by gluing on colored squares and triangles (sketch b).

Simplification Idea: Teacher cuts fringe. Children use stickers, crayons or felt pens to decorate vest.

Enrichment Idea: Children cut own shapes from construction paper.

Pioneer Life: What kind of clothes do you like to wear? Both pioneers and Indians sometimes wore vests made out of leather. They cut a fringe and sewed on brightly-colored beads to decorate their vests. What colors did you choose to decorate your vest?

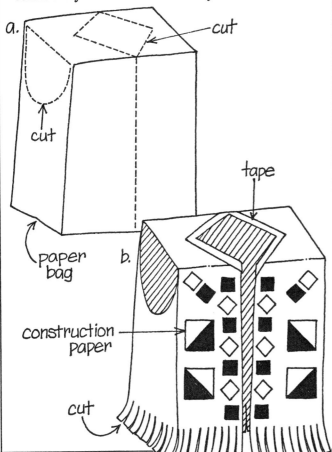

INDIAN HEADBAND
(ONE-DAY PROJECT / 30 MINUTES)

Materials: Tan felt, 1/2-inch (1.25-cm) elastic, scissors, ruler, glue, rickrack and beads in a variety of colors, felt scraps, straight pins, sewing machine and thread. For each child—one safety pin, three sturdy feathers.

Preparation: Cut tan felt into 17×1¼-inch (42.5×3.1-cm) strips—two for each child. Cut elastic into 6-inch (15-cm) lengths—one for each child. Lay two felt strips together and pin (sketch a). Insert end of elastic piece between felt strips 1/2-inch (1.25-cm) deep and pin (sketch b). Use sewing machine set on basting stitch to sew felt strips and elastic together, 1/4-inch (.6-cm) from edge (sketch c). Cut felt scraps into a variety of shapes that will fit onto headband. Cut rickrack into lengths that will fit onto headband.

Instruct each child in the following procedures:
- Use glue to attach felt shapes, rickrack and beads to headband. Let dry.
- Insert feathers between felt strips of headband, pushing end of feather through stitching.
- With teacher's help, use safety pin to join free end of elastic to free end of headband, adjusting to fit child's head.

Pioneer Life: What is something you do well? Many Indians were good at making things like headbands. They worked hard to make beautiful designs. The Indians felt proud when they wore their headbands. You are working hard on your headband! How do you feel when you're wearing it?

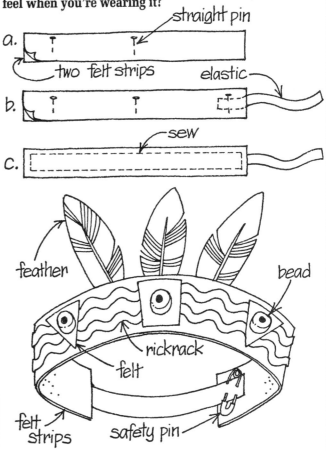

SPOON DOLL
(ONE-DAY PROJECT / 30 MINUTES)

Note: The Spoon Doll will fit into the Rocking Cradle (p. 12).

Materials: Doll Dress and Pants Patterns, gingham or calico and denim fabric, sandpaper, glue, yarn in various colors including brown, scissors, ruler, medium-tip felt pens, fine-toothed saw. For each child—one wooden spoon and one chenille wire.

Preparation: Use saw to cut handles of wooden spoons so spoons stand 9 inches (22.5 cm) tall. For girl doll's hair, cut brown yarn into 5-inch (12.5-cm) lengths—about 40 for each child. For hair ties and belt, cut colorful yarn into 8-inch (20-cm) lengths—three for each child. For boy doll's hair, cut brown yarn into 3-inch (7.5-cm) lengths. Trace Doll Dress Pattern or Shirt and Pants Patterns onto fabric and cut out—one set for each child.

Instruct each child in the following procedures:
- Use sandpaper to sand end of spoon handle.
- Lay the spoon on table, indented side up. Squeeze glue onto the top 1/2-inch (1.25-cm) of spoon face. Lay ends of brown yarn pieces onto glued area (sketch a). Let dry.

- For girl doll, divide hair into two ponytails (sketch b). With teacher's help, tie yarn on each ponytail for bow. For boy doll, glue hair down on back side of spoon.
- Insert spoon through the neck of dress or shirt as in sketch c. Twist chenille wire around handle of the spoon just below the face and secure with glue (sketch c).
- Fold dress or shirt down over arms and body and glue edges of clothes together (sketch d). Let dry.
- Glue pants on front and back of boy doll (sketch f).
- For girl doll, tie yarn around doll and dress for belt (sketch e).
- Use felt pen to draw facial features on doll.

Pioneer Life: **What is your favorite toy? Pioneer children couldn't always go to a store to buy toys. So their parents made toys such as wooden dolls for them to play with. Doll clothes were made from scraps of leftover cloth. Because pioneer children didn't have many toys, the ones they had were very special to them. What name will you give your spoon doll?**

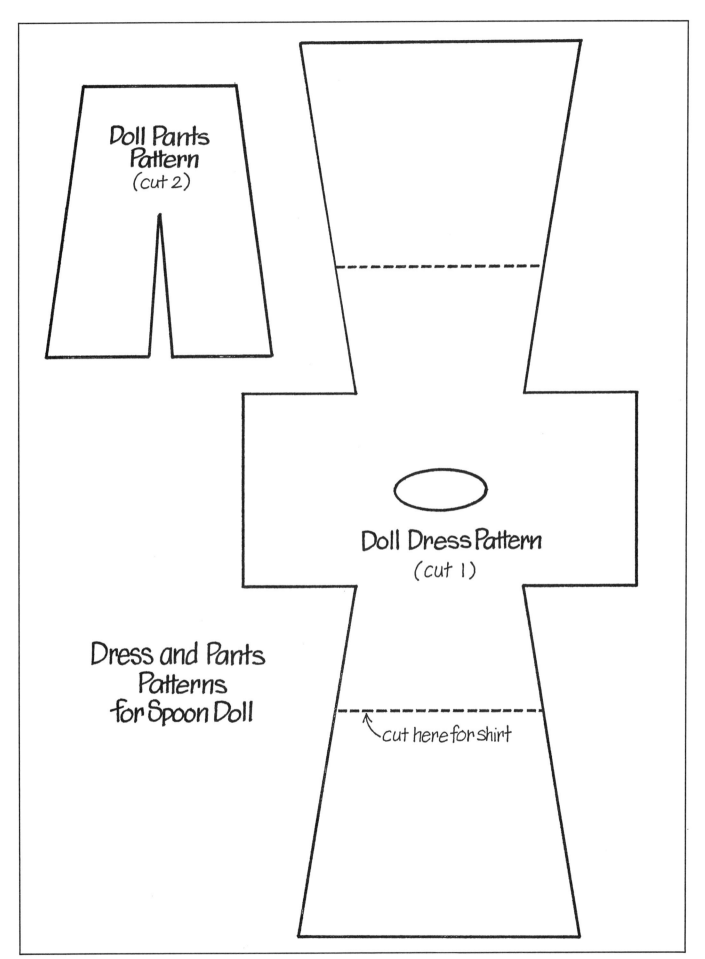

Doll Pants
Pattern
(cut 2)

Doll Dress Pattern
(cut 1)

Dress and Pants
Patterns
for Spoon Doll

cut here for shirt

FLOWER MASK
(ONE-DAY PROJECT / 30 MINUTES)

Materials: Face Opening Pattern, Flower Petal Pattern, yellow tempera paint, shallow pans for paint, sponges, stapler, glue, scissors, pencil, ruler, hole punch, masking tape, brightly-colored construction paper, yarn, newspaper. For each child—two 9-inch (22.5-cm), white paper plates.

Preparation: Trace Flower Petal Pattern onto various colors of construction paper and cut out—ten for each child. Cut out center of one paper plate for each child (sketch a). Place a piece of tape on either side of opening on front of plate, just above center. Use hole punch to punch two holes through tape and plate on each side (sketch b). Center Face Opening Pattern on second plate, trace and cut one for each child (sketch c). Cut yarn into 20-inch (50-cm) lengths—two for each child. Dampen sponges, squeeze out excess water and cut into 2x4-inch (5x10-cm) rectangles. Mix paint to the thickness of heavy cream. Pour paint into shallow pans. Cover work surface with newspaper.

Instruct each child in the following procedures:

- Dip damp sponge into paint and sponge onto back side of plate that has face opening (sketch c). Cover entire surface and let dry.
- Choose ten flower petals. With teacher's help, staple petals to back side of unpainted plate, overlapping petals slightly (sketch d).
- Thread one piece of yarn through each set of holes on the plate and knot on side opposite of the petals (sketch e).
- Squeeze line of glue on front (unpainted) side of painted plate. Lay plate with petals onto glued plate and press together. Make sure yarn ties are aligned at temples of face opening. Let dry.
- Tie Flower Mask on child at back of head.

Enrichment Idea: Allow children to cut out their own petals and decorate with crayons, paint or glue and glitter.

Pioneer Life: (You may want to take your class on a walk outside to look for things God has made. Also, bring in a variety of different flowers for children to look at and touch.) **What are some of the beautiful things God has made? As the pioneers traveled in their covered wagons they saw the colorful flowers that God made. What color is your flower?**

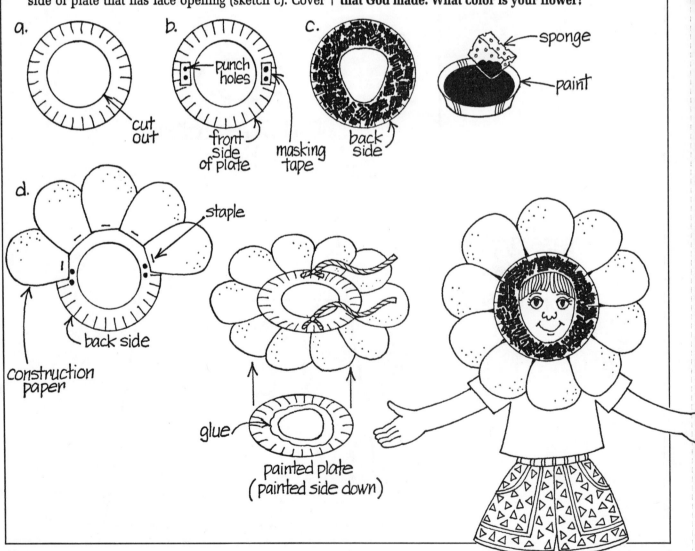

a. cut out

b. punch holes / front side of plate / masking tape

c. back side / sponge / paint

d. staple / back side / construction paper

glue / painted plate (painted side down)

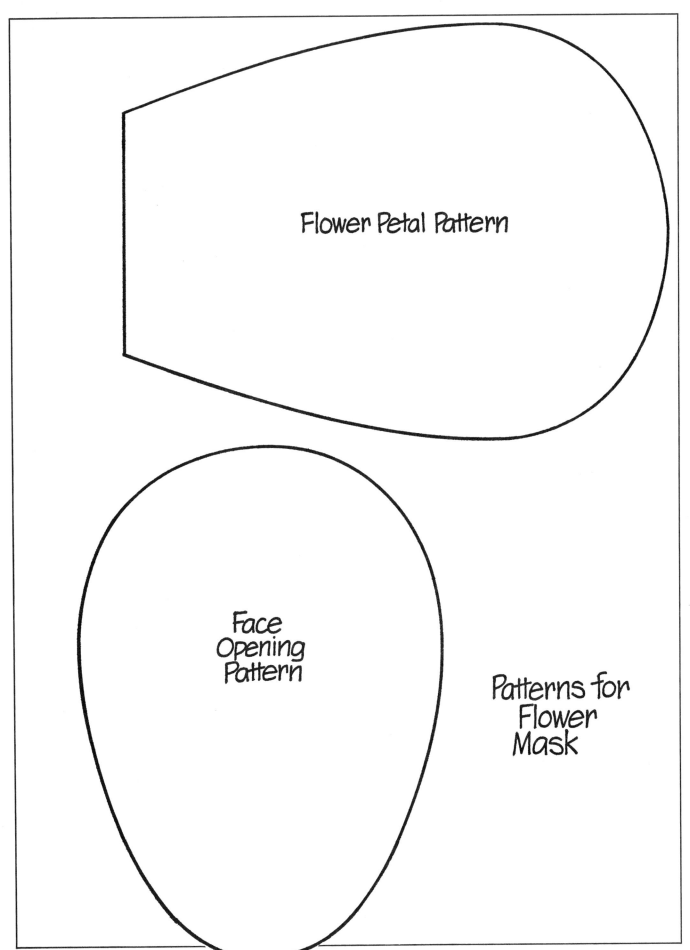

Flower Petal Pattern

Face
Opening
Pattern

Patterns for
Flower
Mask

17

STICK HORSE
(ONE- OR TWO-DAY PROJECT / 60 MINUTES)

Note: This craft requires more teacher preparation and teacher assistance than usual. However, the extra effort involved is well worth it. The Stick Horse is a craft children will enjoy making *and* playing with for months to come.

Materials: Horse Eyelid, Inner Ear and Outer Ear Patterns, polyester fiberfill, felt pen, red, blue, tan and pink felt, 1/2-inch (1.25-cm) cotton cord, 3/4-inch (1.9-cm) dowels, heavy string, craft glue, ruler, scissors, saw. For each child—one men's white sock, two dark-colored 1-inch (2.5-cm) buttons, two dark-colored 5/8-inch (1.5-cm) buttons.

Preparation: Cut dowels into 36-inch (90-cm) lengths. Trace Eyelid and Outer Ear Patterns onto tan felt and cut out—two eyelids and two ears for each child. Trace Inner Ear Pattern onto pink felt and cut out—two for each child. Cut a slit in each outer ear, as shown on pattern. Overlap felt on either side of slit and glue so ear stands up and curves (sketch a). Cut blue felt into 2x12-inch (5x30-cm) strips—one for each child. For mane and forelock, cut red felt into 8x2-inch (20x5-cm) strips—two for each child, and 5x2-inch (12.5x5-cm) strips—five for each child. Cut all red felt strips lengthwise in thirds, stopping 1 inch (2.5-cm) before the end of each strip (sketch b). Cut cord into 5-foot (1.5-m) lengths—one for each child. Wrap ends of cord with tape. Cut string into 1-foot (30-cm) lengths—one for each child.

Instruct each child in the following procedures:
- Stuff foot of sock with fiberfill. Stuff heel and ankle area of sock fuller than the rest (sketch c).
- Place end of dowel in sock and stuff fiberfill around it, leaving 2 inches (5-cm) at bottom without stuffing.
- Squeeze heavy line of glue on the dowel, under sock. With teachers help, wind heavy string tightly around sock and dowel 2 inches (5-cm) from end. Knot string (sketch d).
- Glue inner ears inside outer ears (sketch e). Glue ears to horse.
- Glue the two longer red felt strips to back of neck 2 inches (5-cm) down from ears (sketch f).
- Glue three of the shorter red felt strips to back of head directly behind ears (sketch g).
- Glue two remaining shorter red felt strips to top of head for forelock (sketch h).
- Glue on 1-inch (2.5-cm) buttons for eyes. Glue felt eyelids over eyes (sketch h).
- At the tip of the sock, glue on smaller buttons for nostrils (sketch h).
- Glue blue felt strip around horse's head for bridle.
- With teacher's help, find center of cord and place on bridle (sketch i). Wrap cord around bridle twice and tie once underneath the nose. Draw reins up around back of horse's neck and knot (sketch j).

Pioneer Life: How did you get here today? In pioneer days there were no cars. People walked, rode horses or rode in wagons pulled by oxen. Let's pretend we're pioneers. What is your horse's name? Where will you ride on your horse? Let's stop at this stream and let our horses take a drink. What else can you do to take good care of your horse?

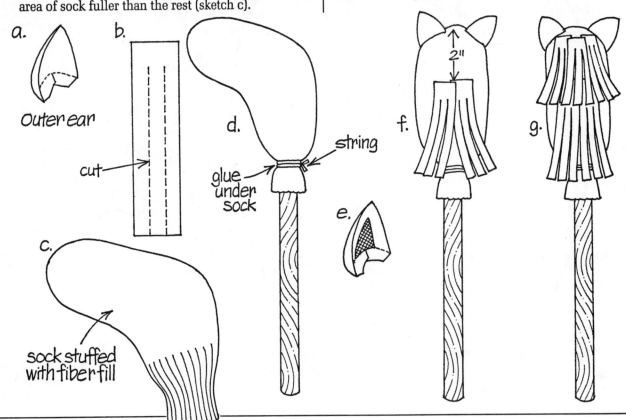

a. Outer ear

b. cut

c. sock stuffed with fiberfill

d. glue under sock / string

e.

f.

2"

g.

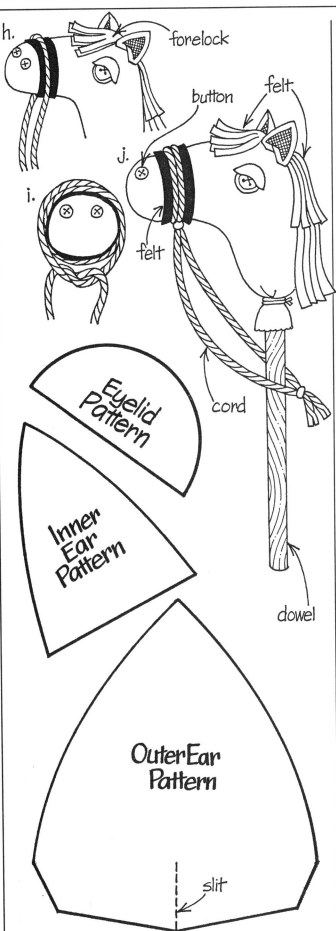

h.

forelock

button

felt

j.

i.

felt

cord

Eyelid Pattern

Inner Ear Pattern

Outer Ear Pattern

dowel

slit

CATERPILLAR CLOTHESPIN MAGNET
(ONE-DAY PROJECT / 30 MINUTES)

Materials: White chenille wires, scissors, ruler, glue. For each child—five 1/2-inch (1.25-cm) green pom-poms, one wooden spring clothespin, one 2-inch (5-cm) fabric leaf, two 4-mm wiggle eyes, one 1×1/4-inch (2.5×.6-cm) magnet. Optional—green tempera paint, paintbrushes.

Preparation: Cut chenille wire into 4-inch (10-cm) pieces—one for each child.

Instruct each child in the following procedures:
- Glue magnet to one side of clothespin (sketch a).
- Glue end of leaf to opposite side of clothespin (sketch a).
- With teacher's help, bend chenille wire to form antennae (sketch b).
- Squeeze line of glue along top of clothespin and over leaf (sketch c).
- Place one pom-pom at end of clothespin for head. Then add chenille wire antennae, followed by remaining four pom-poms to form body.
- Glue two wiggle eyes to pom-pom head. Let entire craft dry.

Enrichment Idea: Before assembling caterpillar, children paint clothespin with green tempera paint.

Pioneer Life: (You may want to bring in a live caterpillar for the children to see and hold. Also, bring in a book showing the life cycle of a caterpillar.) **Pioneer children loved to go exploring. They found all kinds of bugs! They probably liked finding caterpillars! Touch the caterpillar. How does it feel? How is a caterpillar different from other bugs? (It will turn into a butterfly.)**

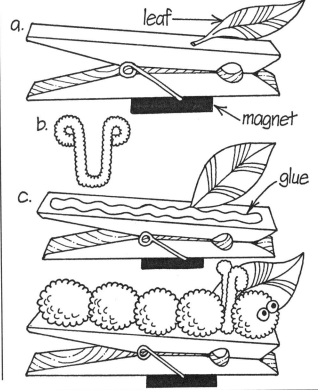

a. leaf

magnet

b.

c. glue

CUP AND BALL GAME
(ONE-DAY PROJECT / 30 MINUTES)

Materials: Yarn, hole punch, scissors, ruler, self-adhesive stickers. For each child—one 1-inch (2.5-cm) colorful wooden bead with hole through it, one brightly-colored plastic cup.

Preparation: Cut yarn into 16-inch (40-cm) lengths—one for each child.

Instruct each child in the following procedures:
- Punch hole in cup near top.
- Decorate cup with stickers.
- With teacher's help, thread one end of yarn through wooden bead and knot twice. Thread other end of yarn through hole in cup and knot twice.
- Hold cup in one hand and try to catch ball in cup.

Simplification Idea: To make game less challenging, shorten length of yarn and increase size of cup.

Pioneer Life: **What games do you like to play? Pioneer children liked to play with a cup and ball game made out of wood. They had contests to see who could get the ball in the cup the most times. Can you get the ball in your cup?**

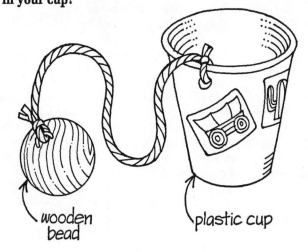

wooden bead

plastic cup

POP-UP PIONEER
(ONE-DAY PROJECT / 30 MINUTES)

Materials: Glue, string, hole punch, fake fur, permanent fine-tip felt pens, solid color fabric (white, tan or brown), gingham fabric, white, tan or brown chenille wires, scissors, ruler, pencil. For each child—one empty, sliding matchbox, two cotton balls, two 4-mm wiggle eyes, seven craft sticks.

Preparation: Cut fake fur into very small pieces to be used as hair and moustaches. Cut string into 17-inch (42.5-cm) lengths—one for each child. Cut solid color fabric into 8-inch (20-cm) squares—one for each child. Cut gingham fabric into 4-inch (10-cm) triangles—one for each child. Cut chenille wires into 8-inch (20-cm) lengths—one for each child.

Instruct each child in the following procedures:
- Separate matchbox from matchbox cover.
- With teacher's help, punch a hole in the center of each side of the matchbox cover (sketch a).
- Thread the string through both holes and knot (sketch a).
- Glue craft sticks to the front of match box cover (sketch d).
- Place two cotton balls in center of fabric square (sketch b). Gather up fabric around cotton balls to form a stuffed "head." To secure head, wrap center of chenille wire twice around pioneer's neck (sketch c). Remaining wire becomes arms. Bend arms to make elbows.
- Glue on fake fur for hair and moustache. Glue on wiggle eyes. Use felt pen to draw nose and mouth.
- Glue gingham fabric around pioneer's neck for bandana.
- Lay pioneer inside matchbox. Slide box into matchbox cover and set upright on flat surface. Pull on both sides of string to make pioneer pop up (sketch d).

Pioneer Life: **What TV program do you like to watch? Pioneer children didn't have TVs. Sometimes they made each other laugh by making puppets and doing puppet shows. Can you do a puppet show with your Pop-Up Pioneer?**

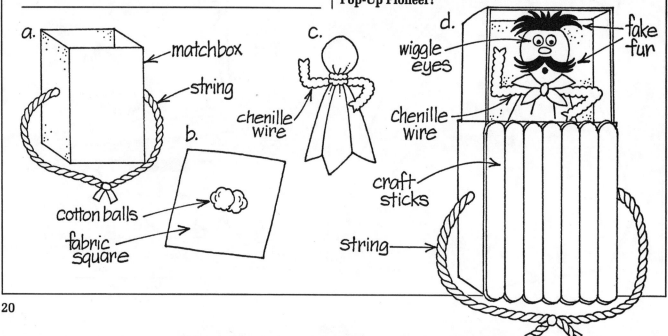

a. matchbox / string

b. cotton balls / fabric square

c. chenille wire

d. wiggle eyes / fake fur / chenille wire / craft sticks / string

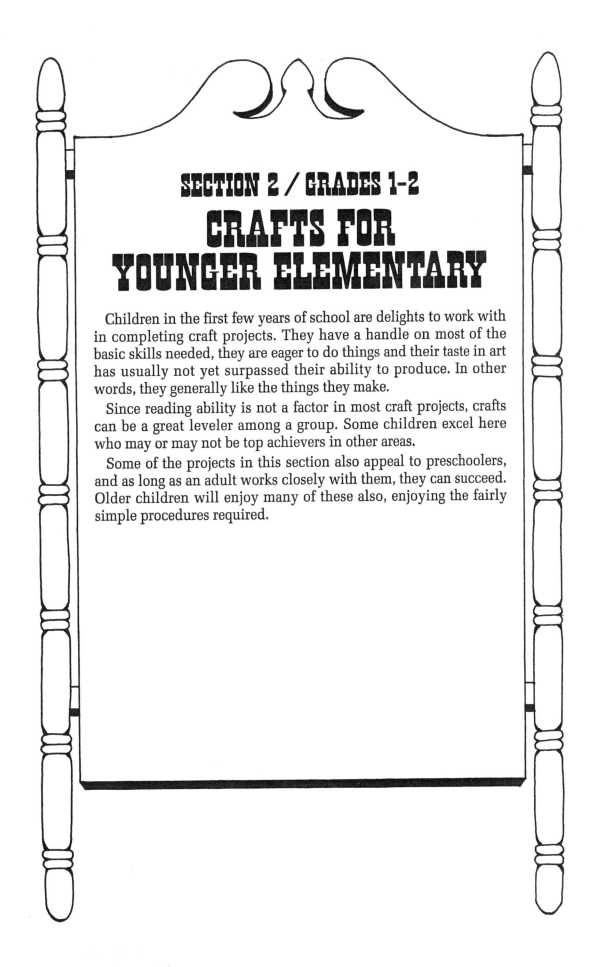

SECTION 2 / GRADES 1-2
CRAFTS FOR YOUNGER ELEMENTARY

Children in the first few years of school are delights to work with in completing craft projects. They have a handle on most of the basic skills needed, they are eager to do things and their taste in art has usually not yet surpassed their ability to produce. In other words, they generally like the things they make.

Since reading ability is not a factor in most craft projects, crafts can be a great leveler among a group. Some children excel here who may or may not be top achievers in other areas.

Some of the projects in this section also appeal to preschoolers, and as long as an adult works closely with them, they can succeed. Older children will enjoy many of these also, enjoying the fairly simple procedures required.

FABRIC CRAYON QUILT SQUARE
(ONE-DAY PROJECT / 30 MINUTES)

Note: You may want to use these squares to make a quilt. See page 7 for quilt instructions. If you are not making a quilt, follow instructions below to make wall hangings from individual squares.

Materials: Fabric crayons (available at fabric or craft supply stores), scissors, ruler, iron, ironing board, muslin, white paper. To make wall hangings—lightweight fusible interfacing, 1/4-inch (.6-cm) diameter dowels, cotton cord, felt yardage, saw, sewing machine, thread.

Preparation: If you will be making a quilt, wash and dry muslin to preshrink. Cut muslin into 9-inch (22.5-cm) squares—one for each child. Cut white paper into 8-inch (20-cm) squares—one for each child. For wall hangings: Cut fusible interfacing into 9-inch (22.5-cm) squares—one for each child. Cut dowels into 12-inch (30-cm) lengths—one for each child. Cut cord into 24-inch (60-cm) lengths—one for each child. Cut felt into 10×12-inch (25×30-cm) rectangles—one for each child. Use sewing machine to stitch a 1/2-inch (1.25-cm) casing for dowel at top of felt piece (sketch c).

Instruct each child in the following procedures:
- Use fabric crayon to trace hand on white paper (sketch a).
- Use fabric crayons to color in hand or add other decorations. (Remember, any lettering must be done backwards.)
- Lay drawing facedown on muslin square. Make sure iron is hot. With teacher's help, iron the back of the paper for approximately 30 seconds to transfer your design from the paper to the muslin square (sketch b).

If you are making a quilt, see page 7. If children are making wall hangings, they follow these procedures:
- Lay interfacing and then muslin square in the center of felt rectangle (sketch c). With teacher's help, iron to fuse the three pieces together.
- Insert dowel into casing.
- Tie cord to each end of dowel to form a hanger (sketch d).

Pioneer Life: **How do you keep warm at night? Pioneers kept warm by using blankets, called quilts, made from scraps of colorful fabric.**

PIONEER CART
(ONE-DAY PROJECT / 30 MINUTES)

Materials: Poster board, pencil, wood-grain self-adhesive paper, scissors, ruler, masking tape, glue, craft knife, nails with large diameter flat head, Spanish moss or Easter grass or straw. For each child—half-gallon cardboard milk carton, two small margarine tub lids, two 3/4-inch (1.9-cm) paper fasteners, tongue depressor.

Preparation: Draw cross pattern onto poster board and cut out (sketch a). Trace cross pattern onto self-adhesive paper—one for each child. Using craft knife, cut each milk carton to a 3-inch (7.5-cm) height (sketch b). Use nail to make a hole on opposite sides of each milk carton, about 3/8 inch (.9-cm) from bottom (sketch b). Use nail to make hole in center of each margarine lid.

Instruct each child in the following procedures:
- Cut out self-adhesive cross.
- Pull backing off self-adhesive cross. Place milk carton on center of cross (sketch c).
- One side at a time, smooth paper up and over top edge of carton until all four sides are covered. Smooth paper to fit snugly around corners.
- From scrap self-adhesive paper, cut six narrow strips to be used as spokes on wheels (margarine lids).
- Pull backing off strips and adhere to inside of lids (sketch d).
- With teacher's help, poke nail through lid and milk carton to reestablish holes.
- On each side of cart, push paper fastener through lid and milk carton. Spread ends of fastener apart to secure in place (sketch e).
- Glue end of tongue depressor to bottom of wagon. Tape in place to reinforce (sketch e).
- Fill cart with Spanish moss, Easter grass or straw.

Pioneer Life: **In pioneer times, the farmers used carts to bring their crops to market. What might the farmers have carried in their carts?**

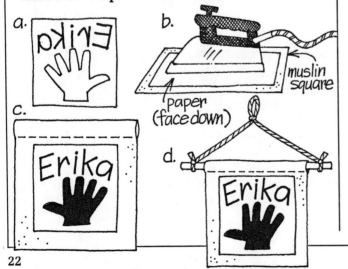

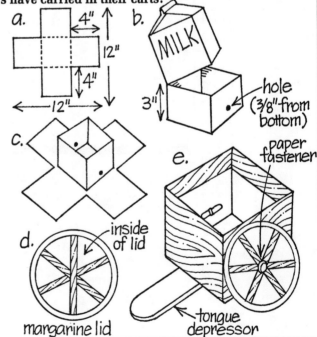

SOD HOUSE
(ONE-DAY PROJECT / 30 MINUTES)

Materials: Clay, small branches or sticks, black markers, ruler, glue, Spanish moss, craft knife, cardboard. For each child—two metal "pop-top" openers from soft drink cans. Optional—small silk or dried flowers, sand, hot glue gun and glue sticks.

Preparation: Week before project—collect assorted sticks and small branches. Spread them out and let dry completely. Use craft knife to cut cardboard into 7×9-inch (17.5×22.5-cm) rectangles—one for each child. Use craft knife to score a line 1 inch (2.5-cm) from bottom edge of cardboard (don't cut all the way through). Fold edge up, making a 90-degree angle (sketch a). This will be the "ground." Glue two "pop-tops" to the back side of each cardboard rectangle to make hangers.

Instruct each child in the following procedures:
- Use black marker to draw a door and window on the cardboard. Color them in (sketch b).
- Break sticks into short pieces to frame door and window. Glue sticks to cardboard (sketch c). (Optional: Teacher uses glue gun to help glue sticks in place. The hot glue dries more quickly and the children

will be able to progress at a faster pace.)
- Break sticks to appropriate lengths and glue just above scored line on cardboard. Press a line of clay above the sticks (sketch d).
- Repeat this process (alternating sticks and clay) until there are about two inches (5 cm) of cardboard showing at top.
- Spread glue over the remaining cardboard at the top. Press Spanish moss onto the glue (sketch e).
- Allow to dry completely. Children may hang their sod houses by the pop-top hangers.

Enrichment Idea: Spread glue on "ground" and sprinkle with sand. Glue small dried or silk flowers to "ground."

Pioneer Life: **What kind of house or apartment do you live in? Pioneers built their own homes out of whatever materials they could find. Some homes were built of wood and sod (soil held together by grass and plant roots). How would you have liked to build a home with your family? What kind of house would you have built?**

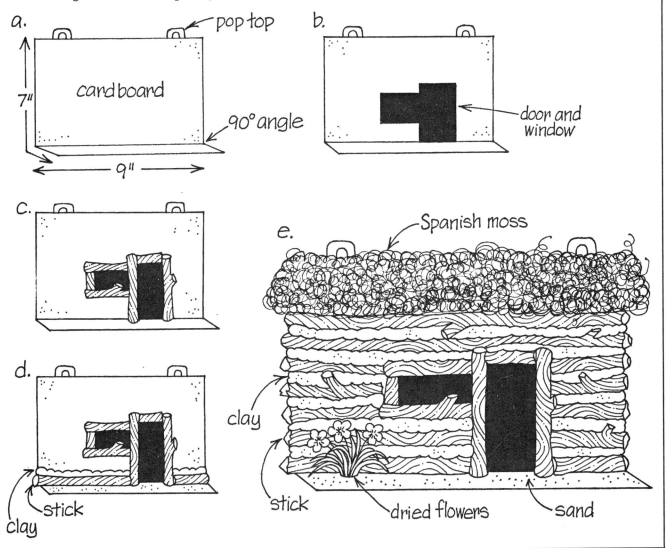

HAND-DIPPED CANDLES
(TWO-DAY PROJECT / 30 MINUTES EACH DAY)

Materials: Paraffin or candle wax, crayons or candle dye, heating unit (stove, hot plate or camp stove), large saucepan, water, candle wicking, scissors, knife, craft sticks, cooking oil, masking tape, felt pens, two large coffee cans, crock pot, old towel, something to hang candles on to dry (towel bar, coat hooks, clothesline). Optional—printed Bible verse, ribbon or torn calico fabric strips.

Preparation: Use scissors to cut craft sticks in half—one half for each child. Cut candle wicking into 18-inch (45-cm) lengths—one for each child. Use tape to attach a craft stick in the center of each length of wick (sketch a).

Clean inside of coffee cans and wipe inside of one can with a thin coat of cooking oil. Use knife to break candle wax or paraffin into chunks small enough to fit easily into the oiled can. Fill the can with wax chunks.

Prepare one center for every five children (sketch b). A teacher or helper must supervise each center.

Heat 3 inches (7.5-cm) of water to boiling in large saucepan. Place can of wax in saucepan and melt to liquid state. Water should remain at low boil. (After all wax has melted, add crayons or dye.)

Pour 2 inches (5-cm) of boiling water into heating crock pot. Transfer the can of wax from saucepan to crock pot.

Fill additional coffee can with room temperature water. Set can of water next to crock pot. Lay old towel next to can of water.

Before beginning project, instruct children about working safely with hot wax.

Instruct each child in the following procedures:
DAY ONE:
- Use felt pen to letter your name on craft stick.
- Grasp craft stick with one hand. Dip both ends of wick into hot wax. Quickly pull wicks out, allowing them to drip over can for a few seconds.
- Dip wicks in can of water.
- Dry wicks by gently wiping them across towel.
- Repeat procedure over and over for about 15 minutes (or until candle is half formed).
- Hang candles to dry until wax is firm (sketch c).
DAY TWO:
- Using previous day's candles, repeat the three steps at the Candle Making Center until desired size is achieved. Hang to dry.
- Remove craft stick.

Note: At first, the wick may curl somewhat. Help children to gently straighten the wick with fingers before dipping into wax again. You may straighten candle immediately after dipping to achieve desired shape.

Enrichment Idea: Letter an appropriate Bible verse on a strip of paper. Wrap the paper around the candles. Then tie candles together with ribbon or strips of calico fabric (sketch d).

Pioneer Life: **Is your room dark at night? In pioneer days there were no electric lights, so at night it was very dark—everywhere! If a pioneer family wanted to have light, they made a fire in the fireplace and lit candles around the room. Pioneers had to be very careful when they used candles. Why do you think it is important to be careful with candles?**

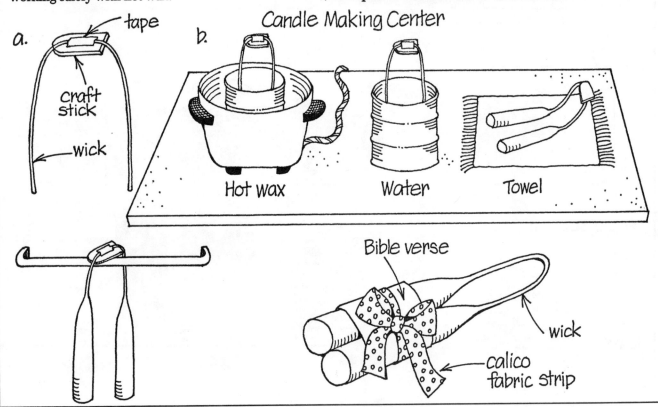

a. tape
craft stick
wick

Candle Making Center
b.
Hot wax   Water   Towel

Bible verse
wick
calico fabric strip

PIE PAN PUNCH
(ONE- OR TWO-DAY PROJECT / 60 MINUTES)

Materials: Apple Pattern, tagboard, scissors, pencil, ruler, hammers, awls or nails with big, flat heads, masking tape, red, green and brown gloss enamel paints, paintbrushes, small containers for paint, paint thinner, jars, old rags, scrap wood, black permanent markers, glue, red yarn. For each child—one 9-inch (22.5-cm) aluminum pie pan, one aluminum pop-top opener from a soft drink can, one paint shirt.

Preparation: Trace Apple Pattern onto tagboard and cut out. Trace around bottom of pie pan onto tagboard and cut out—one circle for each child. Trace Apple Pattern onto the center of each tagboard circle. Use felt pen to indicate awl marks (sketch a). Cut yarn into 32-inch (80-cm) lengths—three for each child. Cut additional yarn into 4-inch (10-cm) lengths—one for each child. Use one long and one short piece of yarn to make a simple yarn bow—one for each child (sketches b and c). Pour paint into small containers.

Instruct each child in the following procedures:
- Review safety rules about use of hammer, awls or nails, and paint that "won't come out!" Put on paint shirt.
- Tape tagboard to inside of pie pan (sketch d).
- Place pie pan on piece of wood. Using a hammer and awl or nail, punch every hole in the pattern (sketch e). Make sure nail goes through tagboard and pie pan. Remove pattern and tape.
- Paint design inside apple shape. Let dry. (Teachers/helpers—clean brushes with paint thinner.)
- Place a line of glue around the entire lip of pie pan. Glue two 32-inch (80-cm) pieces of yarn around the perimeter of pie pan, beginning and ending at the top of pan.
- Glue yarn bow to the top center of pie pan.
- Use black markers to letter "Let's Share" and add detail to design on pie pan (sketch f).
- Glue pop-top opener to the back of pan for hanger. Let dry.

Pioneer Life: **Have you ever gone on a long trip with your family? What did you do when you were hungry? As the pioneers traveled west, they couldn't stop at a restaurant for a hamburger. There were no restaurants in the wilderness. So they had to carry food with them. Many times, they shared food with other travelers. Sometimes they couldn't eat as much as they wanted because they had to make sure the food lasted for the whole trip. When is a time you shared your food?**

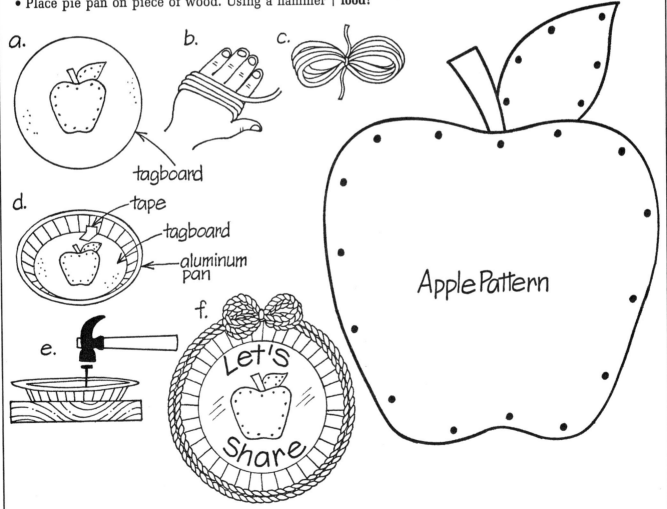

a.

b.

c.

tagboard

d.

tape

tagboard

aluminum pan

e.

f.

Let's Share

Apple Pattern

CANOE
(ONE-DAY PROJECT / 30 MINUTES)

Materials: Canoe Pattern, tan construction paper, wood-grain self-adhesive paper, brown yarn, scissors, ruler, stapler and staples, transparent tape, hole punches, photocopier.

Preparation: Cut self-adhesive paper into 5×12-inch (12.5×30-cm) rectangles—one for each child. Photocopy Canoe Pattern onto tan construction paper—one for each child. Cut yarn into 4-foot (120-cm) lengths. Attach two lengths together by wrapping a piece of tape around each end (sketch a)—one for each child.

Instruct each child in the following procedures:

- Pull backing off self-adhesive paper and apply to back of construction paper (sketch b).
- Use scissors to cut out Canoe Pattern outlined on front of construction paper.
- Lightly fold the canoe in half lengthwise, matching ends. Staple ends together (sketch c).
- Use hole punch to punch holes along top sides of canoe (sketch d).
- Thread yarn through two holes at one end of the canoe (sketch d). Make sure there is an equal amount of yarn on either side of the canoe and tie a knot in the center (sketch e).
- Thread yarn through holes on each side of canoe (sketch f).
- Tie yarn together in a double knot at opposite end of canoe. Cut off excess yarn.

Pioneer Life: Have you ever ridden in a canoe? For us, riding in a canoe is a special treat. For Indians and pioneers who lived near rivers, canoes were a common way of getting around. They traveled in canoes to go hunting, exploring, trading and visiting.

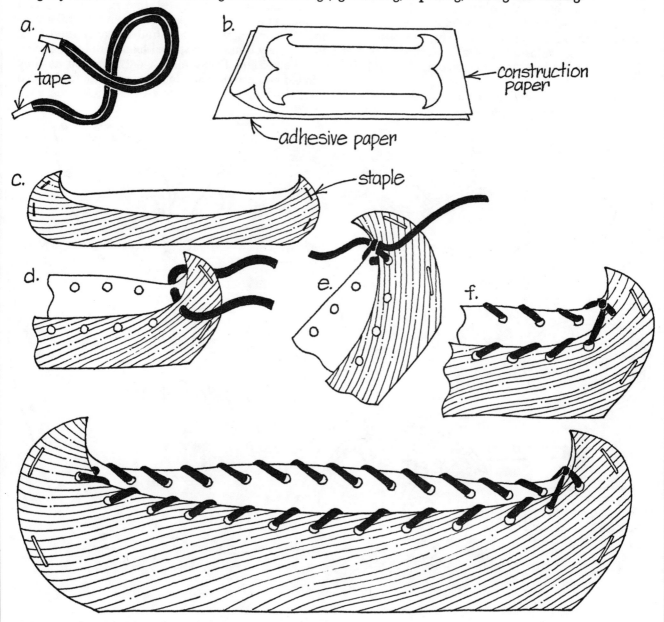

a. tape

b. construction paper

adhesive paper

c. staple

d.

e.

f.

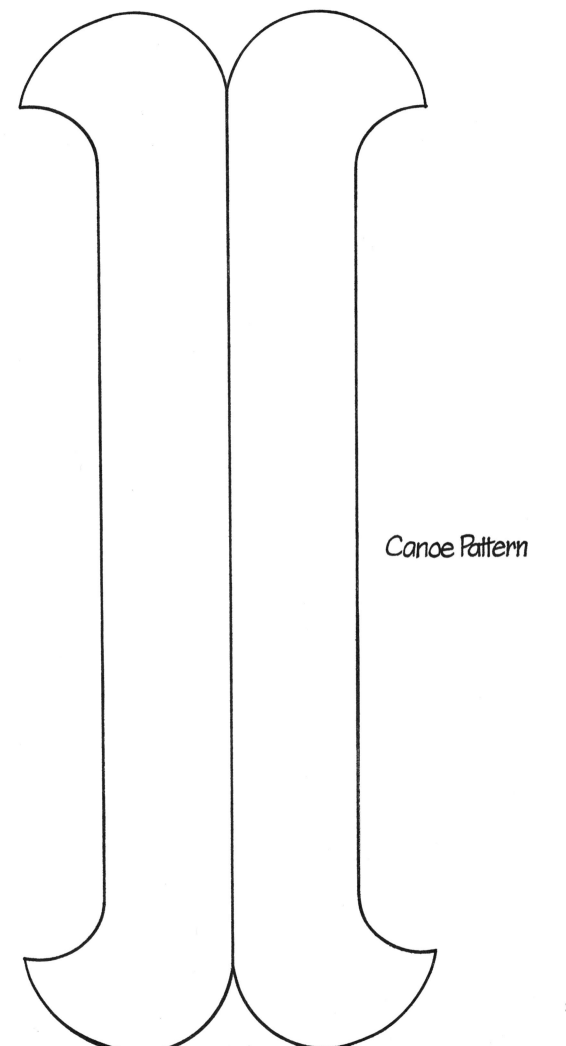

Canoe Pattern

27

PAPER PLATE BUFFALO
(ONE- OR TWO-DAY PROJECT / 60 MINUTES)

Materials: Head, Horn, Tail, Front Legs and Back Legs Patterns, lightweight cardboard, pencil, ruler, black marker, brown watercolor paint, small containers for water and glue, water, paintbrushes, brown tissue paper, brown and tan construction paper, scissors, glue. For each child—one 6-inch (15-cm) white paper plate, one 9-inch (22.5-cm) white paper plate, two 20-mm wiggle eyes, pencil with eraser.

Preparation: Trace Patterns onto lightweight cardboard and cut out. Trace Horn Pattern onto beige construction paper—two for each child. Trace Head, Tail and Legs Patterns onto brown construction paper—one set for each child.

Use black marker to draw nostrils, mouth and feet lines where indicated. (Optional: Patterns may be photocopied onto construction paper.)

Cut brown tissue paper into 1-inch (2.5-cm) squares. Fill containers with water for painting. Pour small amount of glue into additional containers.

Instruct each child in the following procedures:
- Paint the back side of each plate with brown watercolor paint. Let dry.
- Cut out traced pattern pieces.

- Glue head piece onto painted side of smaller paper plate.
- Glue wiggle eyes to head.
- Glue the right horn under the rim of small plate (sketch a). Glue left horn to top side of plate.
- Place pencil eraser in center of a tissue paper square. Bring edges of paper up around pencil (sketch b). Dip end of paper into glue. Transfer tissue paper onto small paper plate, attaching it to buffalo's head (sketch c). Continue until plate is covered.
- Glue tail, front legs and back legs to the large plate (sketch d).
- Glue head to body.

Simplification Idea: To shorten craft time, teacher precuts Horn, Tail, Head and Leg pieces.

Pioneer Life: **Have you ever seen a buffalo? Pioneers saw many buffalo as they traveled in their covered wagons. Both Indians and pioneers killed buffalo and ate the meat, made clothing from the skin and used the bones for cooking utensils. After a while, there were not many buffalo left because so many were killed. Today we take care of buffalo to make sure there will always be buffalo on the earth.**

a.

b. pencil

tissue paper

c.

d.

PaperPlate Buffalo Patterns

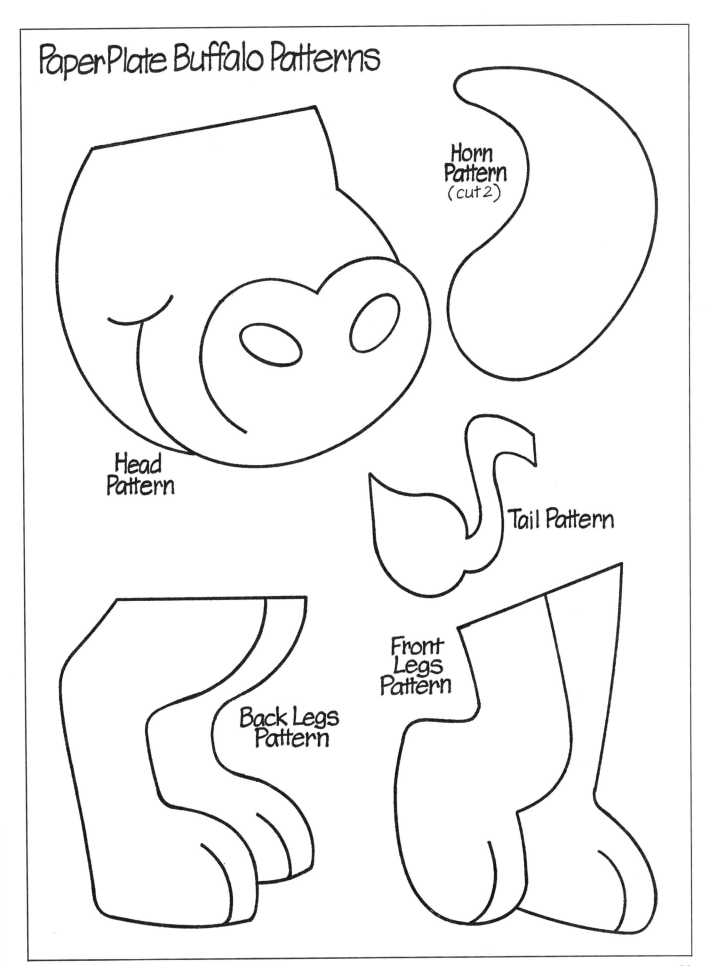

Horn Pattern
(cut 2)

Head Pattern

Tail Pattern

Back Legs Pattern

Front Legs Pattern

KITE

(ONE- OR TWO-DAY PROJECT / 60 MINUTES)

Note: This craft requires more teacher preparation and teacher assistance than usual. It will work best with a small group of children or as a special one-to-one, parent-child project.

Materials: Scissors, paste (white glue will cause puckering), tempera paints, sponges, shallow containers, ruler, hot glue gun and glue sticks, black permanent marker, calico or gingham fabric, transparent tape, butcher paper at least 36 inches (90-cm) in width, 1/4-inch (.6-cm) diameter dowels, fine-toothed saw. For each child—one spool of string.

Preparation: Cut sponges into a variety of shapes (square, triangle, heart, circle). Cut dowels into 30-inch (75-cm) lengths—one for each child. Cut additional dowels into 36-inch (90-cm) lengths—one for each child. Cut a 1/4-inch (.6-cm) slit in the ends of each dowel (sketch a). Use black marker to make a black dot on the center of each shorter dowel (sketch a). Cut a slight notch 1/2-inch (1.25-cm) from bottom of each longer dowel (sketch b). Make a black dot 9 inches (22.5-cm) from the top of each longer dowel (sketch b).

Cut fabric into 1×6-inch (2.5×15-cm) strips—six for each child. For each child—cut paper to make a 36×40-inch (90×100-cm) kite covering (sketch c). Cut corners off each kite covering as shown in sketch. If you do not have a large enough piece of paper, attach two pieces together by overlapping paper two inches in the center and taping (sketch d).

For each child—cut string into three 48-inch (120-cm) lengths, one 42-inch (105-cm) length and one 20-inch (50-cm) length. Pour the paint into shallow containers.

Instruct each child in the following procedures:

- To decorate the front side of kite: Dip sponge in paint and press lightly onto kite covering. Repeat, using a variety of colors until majority of the kite is painted. Let dry.
- To make the kite frame: Place the shorter dowel crosswise with the black dot up. Teacher uses glue gun to put a spot of glue on the black dot. Immediately place the longer dowel lengthwise on the glued spot, matching black dots. Hold dowels together until glue cools and hardens. Wrap 20-inch (50-cm) string around the intersection of crossed dowels to reinforce and secure. Tie a knot and cut off excess string (sketch e).
- **Note:** When the following instructions say "attach string to dowel," do the following—place string securely into notch on dowel (sketch f). Tie string around stick (sketch g).
- Attach 48-inch (120-cm) string to bottom of lengthwise stick and tie a knot. Pull string taut and attach to one end of crosswise dowel. Continue process of framing kite until you reach the bottom of kite again. Attach string at notch on bottom of lengthwise dowel again and tie a knot (sketch h).
- Lay the kite frame on the undecorated side of paper covering.
- Spread paste along outer edges of paper. Fold edges over the string and reinforce with tape (sketch i).
- To make bridle: Attach ends of 48-inch (120-cm) length of string to ends of lengthwise dowel. Knot at both ends. (The string will be loose, not taut.)
- Attach the 42-inch (105-cm) bridle string to crosswise dowel and knot at both ends.
- To make the kite tail: Tie a 48-inch length of string to the bottom of the kite. Tie six fabric strips to the string at 6-inch (15-cm) intervals.
- Tie the end of remaining spool of string (flying string) to the intersection of the two bridle strings. (Note: If you have trouble flying the kite, move the flying string up or down on the longer bridle string until it is adjusted correctly and will fly.)

Pioneer Life: What is your favorite toy? Pioneer children enjoyed making and flying kites a lot like the ones we are making.

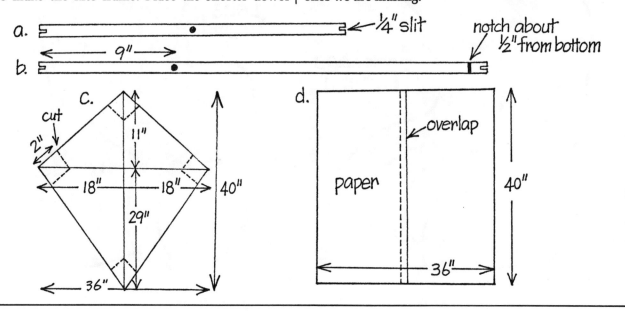

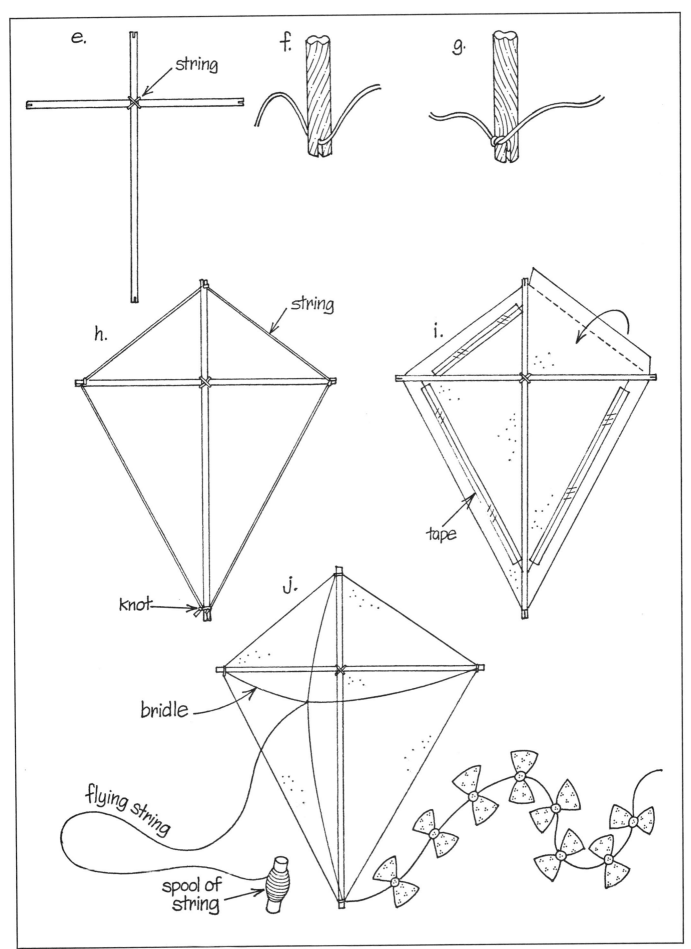

e.

string

f.

g.

h.

string

i.

tape

knot

j.

bridle

flying string

spool of string

TWISTED-YARN BELT
(ONE-DAY PROJECT / 30 MINUTES)

Materials: Yarn in a variety of colors, scissors, measuring stick.

Preparation: Cut yarn into 3-yard ((2.7-cm) lengths—four for each child.

Instruct each child in the following procedures:

- Choose four lengths of yarn. Tie four lengths of yarn together with a knot at each end (sketch a).
- Choose a partner to work with. Partners stand facing one another, holding ends of yarn and pulling it taut (sketch b).
- Each child twists the yarn clockwise (to the right) until the yarn is tightly twisted and it begins to "kink."
- Give one child both ends of the yarn to hold. (Make sure yarn stays twisted.) The other child pulls on the center of the yarn and then lets go. The yarn should twist itself together, forming a yarn rope (sketch c). (If yarn does not twist, repeat previous step, twisting yarn even tighter.)
- Tie one knot 2 inches (5-cm) from the previously tied knots, joining the yarn together (sketch d). Cut off original, smaller knots and untwist yarn to form tassel.
- Tie another knot 2 inches (5-cm) from the opposite end. Then cut through the yarn at the end of the loop to form a tassel on that end.
- Repeat process to make belt for the second child.

Pioneer Life: **What is something you are good at? How did you learn to (play the piano)? Indians were especially good at using yarn to make brightly-colored rugs and clothing. Indian children learned by watching the women as they made their colorful designs. What colors did you choose for your belt?**

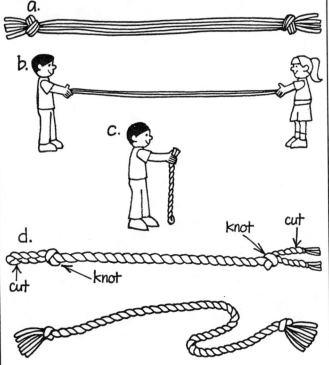

PIONEER DOLL
(ONE- OR TWO-DAY PROJECT / 60 MINUTES)

Materials: Pioneer Girl and Pioneer Boy Patterns, poster board, butcher paper, paper clips, white tissue paper or fiberfill, glue, scissors, yarn, felt pens, staplers and staples, pencil, measuring stick, old buttons, scraps of fabric, wallpaper, gift wrap, lace, ribbon, etc. For each child—two 15-mm wiggle eyes.

Preparation: Cut poster board into four 16×20-inch (37.5×50-cm) sheets. On each sheet of poster board, use a pencil and measuring stick to divide area into 2-inch (5-cm) squares. Then enlarge the Pioneer Boy Pattern by copying each square from the Pattern grid onto one sheet of poster board. Cut out. Enlarge Pioneer Girl Pattern in same way and cut out. Trace Girl and Boy Patterns onto sheets of butcher paper and cut out—two Girl Patterns for each girl and two Boy Patterns for each boy. (Each child needs one piece for front of doll and one for back.) Use paper clips to clip sets together. Enlarge Clothes Patterns (Hat, Shirt, Vest, Pants, Bonnet, Dress) onto two remaining sheets of poster board and cut out—one set for every four or five children.

Instruct each child in the following procedures:

- Glue wiggle eyes on face.
- Use felt pens to draw mouth, hair and other details.
- Trace appropriate Clothes Patterns onto fabric, gift wrap or wallpaper. Cut out and glue onto front of doll.
- Use buttons, lace, ribbon, additional fabric, paper and felt pens to add embellishments to doll.
- With the decorated side out, match the front to the back of the doll. Staple the front and back feet together, about 1/4-inch (.6-cm) from edge. Loosely crumple tissue paper and gently stuff it into the stapled feet section. Staple leg section, then stuff. Continue until entire doll is stapled and stuffed.

Enrichment Idea: Children decorate back of doll.

Pioneer Life: **Pioneers didn't have easy lives. They worked very hard making their own tools, wagons, homes, furniture, clothes and food. But pioneer life was exciting, too, because these people were traveling to new places, to settle down and start new lives. Where would you like to travel?**

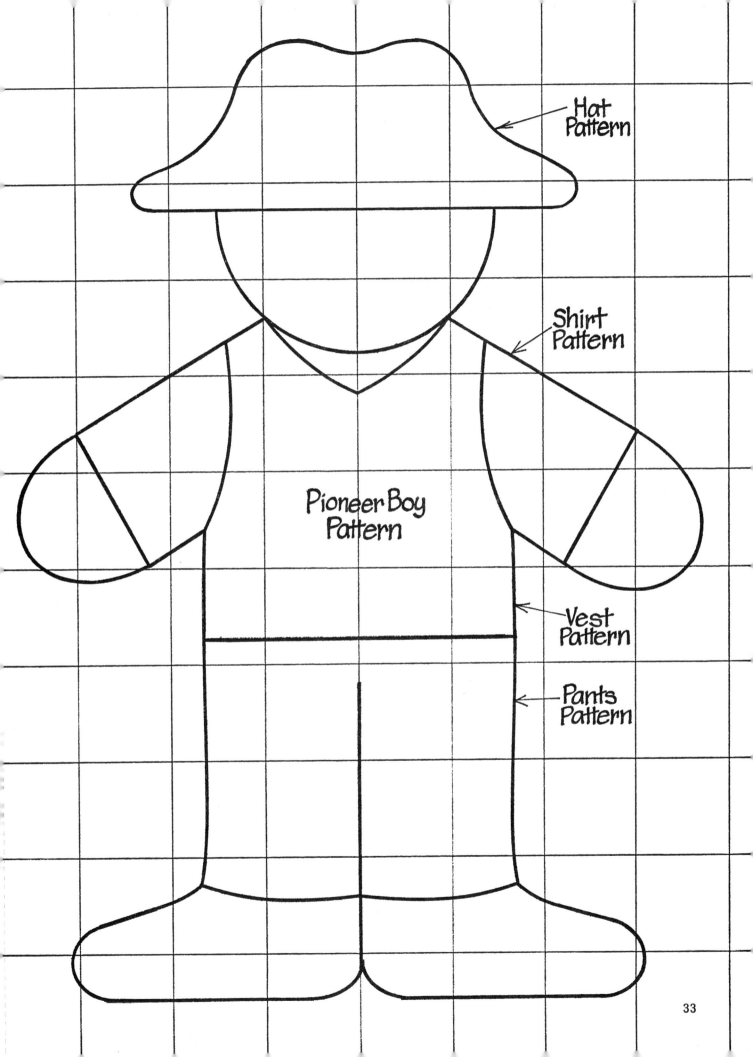

Hat
Pattern

Shirt
Pattern

Pioneer Boy
Pattern

Vest
Pattern

Pants
Pattern

33

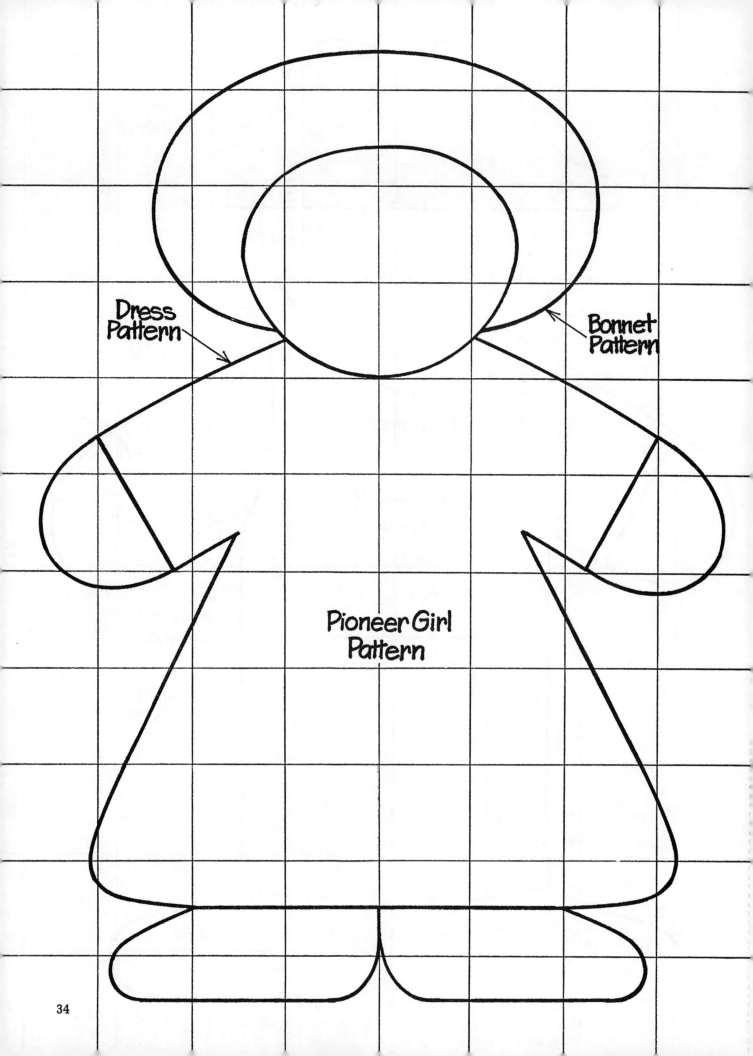

Dress
Pattern

Bonnet
Pattern

Pioneer Girl
Pattern

34

SECTION 3 / GRADES 3-6
CRAFTS FOR OLDER ELEMENTARY

Trying to plan craft projects for older children has driven many teachers prematurely gray. The challenge is that while these children have well-developed skills to complete projects, they also have well-developed preferences about what they want to do. Thus a project that may challenge their abilities may be scorned because it somehow is not appealing to these young sophisticates. Then the next project will seem juvenile to the adult, but will click with the kids!

There's no justice! And a sense of humor surely helps. One helpful device is to filter a craft idea through a panel of experts—two or three sixth graders. If they like it, chances are the rest of the group will, also. Then, the better you get to know your particular students, the better your batting average will be. And most of the time, most of the group will thoroughly enjoy the projects in this section. They have been tested under fire and came out with colors flying and only a few tatters.

FABRIC PAINT QUILT SQUARE
(ONE-DAY PROJECT / 30 MINUTES)

Note: You may want to use these squares to make a quilt. See page 7 for quilt instructions. If you are not making a quilt, follow instructions below to make pillows from individual squares. The pillow is a two-day project—30 minutes each day.

Materials: Muslin, fabric paints, paintbrushes, containers for water, pencils, rulers, scissors, newspapers. To make pillows—needles, thread, polyester fiberfill, straight pins.

Preparation: Wash and dry muslin to preshrink. Cut muslin into 9-inch (22.5-cm) squares—one for each child. Cover tables with newspaper. To make pillows—cut one additional muslin square for each child.

Instruct each child in the following procedures:
- Use ruler and pencil to draw a 1/2-inch (1.25-cm) border on one muslin square (sketch a).
- Use pencil to lightly draw a design within borders on muslin square.
- Use fabric paints to paint design on muslin square (sketch b). Rinse paintbrush thoroughly.
- Allow to dry for at least four hours. Then adult should iron back of quilt square to set paint.
  If you are making a quilt, see page 7. If children are making pillows, they follow these procedures:
- Use ruler and pencil to draw a 1/2-inch (1.25-cm) border on back side of painted muslin square. (This will be your stitching line.)
- Lay painted muslin square facedown on additional muslin square and pin together (sketch c).
- Thread a needle and knot the thread. Stitch around the square, on stitching line, leaving an opening on one side (sketch d). Remove pins.
- Use scissors to trim corners of square. Turn pillow right side out and stuff with fiberfill.
- Stitch pillow opening closed.

Enrichment Idea: Photocopy Quilt Square Designs on page 9—one for every two children. Children paint authentic quilt square designs on their quilt squares.

Pioneer Life: Pioneer women enjoyed working on quilts together. What projects do you enjoy working on with your friends?

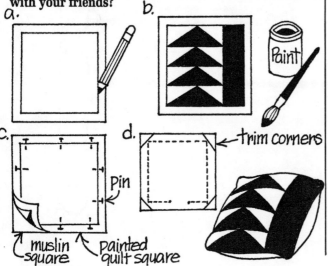

LOG CABIN PHOTO FRAME
(ONE-DAY PROJECT / 30 MINUTES)

Materials: Instant camera and film, glue, ruler, cardboard, scissors. For each child—11 tongue depressors. Optional—felt pens, regular camera and film.

Preparation: Cut cardboard into 5½-inch (13.75-cm) squares—one for each child. Take instant snapshots of small groups of students—one for each child. Optional: Use a regular camera to take photos in advance and have pictures developed in time to complete craft.

Instruct each child in the following procedures:
- Arrange five tongue depressors as shown in sketch a. Glue horizontal piece on top of four vertical pieces.
- Glue on the remaining four tongue depressors (sketch b). Let dry.
- Glue two tongue depressors to back to form roof (sketch c).
- Glue photo facedown on back of frame.
- Glue cardboard square to back of frame for a finished look.

Enrichment Idea: Use felt pen to letter an appropriate Bible verse on front of frame. Draw other decorations if desired.

Pioneer Life: Do you have a favorite photograph of your family? When was it taken? In pioneer days not many people owned cameras. A person who had a photograph of his or her family took very good care of it because it wouldn't be easy to get another one. A pioneer might take out the photograph and look at it for a long time, remembering the good times he or she had with family or friends. Who is in your photo? What good time does your photo remind you of?

COVERED WAGON

(ONE- OR TWO-DAY PROJECT / 60 MINUTES)

Note: This craft requires more teacher preparation and teacher assistance than usual. However, the extra effort involved is well worth it. The Covered Wagon is a project children can be proud of and keep for a long time. Also, the Covered Wagon can be used with Pioneer Folks (page 40).

Materials: White sheeting or white cotton fabric, tagboard, bender board in 3⅜-inch (8.4-cm) width (available at garden supply stores), 1/4-inch (.6-cm) diameter wooden dowels, 1/4-inch (.6-cm) plywood, glue, hot glue gun and glue sticks, ruler, sandpaper, scissors, handsaw, band saw, electric drill with 3/8-inch (.9-cm) bit. For each child—one wooden tongue depressor and four thumbtacks. Optional: Purchase 2¾-inch (6.9-cm) wooden wheels at a craft store—four for each child. If ready-made wheels are purchased, you will not need the plywood, drill and band saw.

Preparation: Cut sheeting into 10x12-inch (25x30-cm) rectangles—one for each child. Use band saw to cut 2¾-inch (6.9-cm) circles from plywood—four for each child. Drill a 3/8-inch (.9-cm) hole in center of each circle.

Cut bender board into 8-inch (20-cm) lengths— three for each child. Cut additional bender board into 3½-inch (8.75-cm) lengths—two for each child. Cut dowels into 4½-inch (11.25-cm) lengths—two for each child. Cut tagboard into 1x18-inch (2.5x45-cm) strips— three for each child.

Instruct each child in the following procedures:

- With teacher's assistance, use hot glue gun to glue longer pieces of bender board together to form a U shape (sketch a).
- Glue shorter pieces of bender board to ends of U shape to form a wagon bed (sketch b). Hold in place while glue dries.
- Glue tagboard strips across sheeting for wagon top (sketch c). Fold ends of sheet over outer strips and glue in place.
- Glue dowels to bottom of wagon, 1½ inches (3.75-cm) from front and back (sketch d).
- Glue end of tongue depressor to bottom of wagon (sketch d).
- Use sandpaper to sand wheels.
- Attach wagon top to wagon by gluing ends of tagboard strips to inside edges of wagon.
- Place wheels on dowel ends and secure by pressing a thumbtack on the end of each dowel.

Pioneer Life: Have you and your family ever moved to a new house? Why? The pioneers were people who wanted to move to a new place because they wanted a better life. Each family packed all they owned into a covered wagon which was pulled by horses or oxen. Many times covered wagons traveled together, forming a wagon train. Each night they stopped and circled the wagons. The families cooked food and spent time together safely inside the circle. The next day the wagon train headed out again across the prairie toward a new home. What would you like about traveling in a covered wagon? Let's use our covered wagons to form a wagon train.

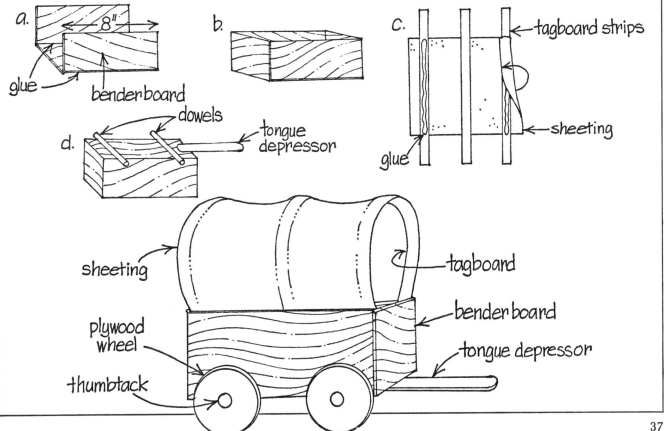

JOURNAL
(ONE- OR TWO-DAY PROJECT / 60 MINUTES)

Materials: Burlap, cardboard, white paper, glue, needles, thread, scissors, ruler, 2-inch (5-cm) wide colored tape. Optional—felt scraps, paper cutter.

Preparation: Cut cardboard into 6×8-inch (15×20-cm) pieces—two for each child. Cut white paper into 7×11-inch (17.5×27.5-cm) sheets—eight for each child. Cut burlap into 8×10-inch (20×25-cm) pieces—two for each child. Cut tape into 16-inch lengths—one for each child.

Instruct each child in the following procedures:
- Fold stack (eight sheets) of white paper in half and then open again. Use needle to poke five holes on crease line (sketch a).
- Thread needle and knot thread twice at the end. Sew paper together, going up through hole *a*, down through hole *b*, up through hole *c* and so on to hole *e* (sketch b). Then continue sewing until you have gone back through each hole arriving at hole *a*. Knot thread twice and cut.
- Glue each cardboard piece to the center of a burlap piece (sketch c).
- Fold four corners of burlap over onto cardboard and glue (sketch d). Fold remaining edges of burlap over onto cardboard and glue (sketch e). Let dry.

- Lay burlap covers facedown on center of length of tape, leaving 1/4-inch (.6-cm) between covers (sketch f).
- Fold ends of tape over to meet in center.
- Glue first page of journal onto inside of front cover, covering up raw edges of burlap. Glue last page to inside of back cover.

Enrichment Idea: Cut out shapes or letters from felt and glue to front cover of journal. Suggest children use journals to record events; thoughts; feelings; write stories; write poetry; draw pictures or collect autographs.

Simplification Idea: Children staple pages together instead of sewing.

Pioneer Life: What do you do at home in the evening? In pioneer days, some people wrote in journals, using only a fire or candle for light. They wrote about what they had done that day, what made them happy and what made them sad. When a pioneer girl finished writing, she might hide her journal in a safe place where no one else would find it—maybe in a corner of the covered wagon or under the bed in her log-cabin home. What will you write about in your journal? Can you think of a good place to keep it?

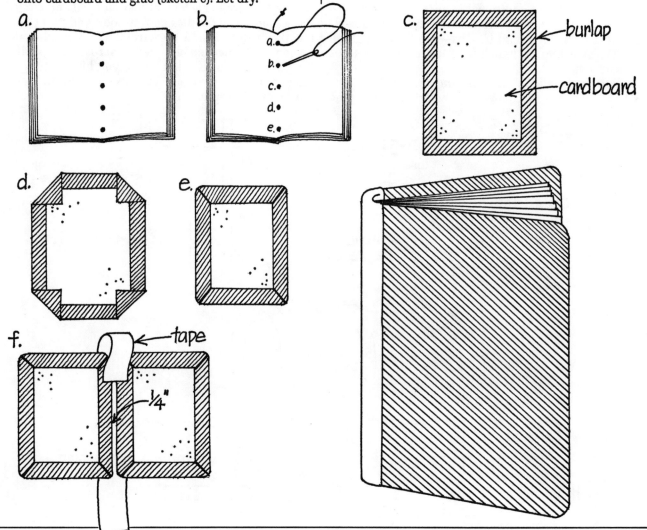

BEESWAX CANDLE AND HOLDER
(ONE- OR TWO-DAY PROJECT / 60 MINUTES)

Materials: Beeswax honeycomb sheets and candle wicking (found in craft supply stores or mail order catalogs), knife, cutting board, scissors, salt, flour, mixing spoon, mixing bowl, water, baking sheets, hot pads, aluminum foil, oven. Optional—acrylic paint, paintbrushes, containers for water, clear acrylic spray.

Preparation: Use knife to cut beeswax into 6×10-inch (15×25-cm) sheets—one for each child. Cut wicking into 11-inch (27.5-cm) lengths—one for each child. Make a sample candle following directions below. Cut aluminum foil into 4-inch (10-cm) squares—two for each child. Crumple each foil piece to approximate diameter of candle. To make salt/flour dough for candle holder: Mix one part flour with one part salt. Add water and mix until you have a dough-like consistency. Separate dough into fist-sized lumps—one for each child.

Instruct each child in the following procedures:
FOR CANDLE HOLDER:
- Use a small amount of dough to make a flat circle about 2 inches (5-cm) in diameter (sketch a).
- Roll remaining dough to make a rope about 16-inches (40-cm) long (sketch b).
- Stand crumpled aluminum foil piece in center of dough circle. Coil dough rope around foil until only five or six inches (12.5 or 15-cm) are left uncoiled (sketch c). Fold uncoiled dough in half and press in place at top and bottom of candle holder to form handle (sketch d).

- Place additional crumpled piece of aluminum foil inside handle. The aluminum foil will help handle retain shape while baking (sketch e).
- Place holder on baking sheet and bake at 350 degrees Fahrenheit for 45 minutes. Remove aluminum foil and let cool.

FOR CANDLE:
- Lay wick along longer edge of beeswax sheet (sketch f).
- Place hands on beeswax sheet for several seconds. (Body heat will soften the beeswax and cause it to roll without cracking.) Roll beeswax sheet around wick as tightly as possible (sketch g).
- Seal edge of candle by pressing briefly onto a warmed baking sheet (sketch h).
- Place candle in holder.

Simplification Idea: Use air-drying clay to make candle holders.

Enrichment Idea: Paint candle holder and spray with acrylic spray.

Pioneer Life: Is your room dark at night? How dark is the street you live on? In pioneer days there was no electricity, so at night it was very dark—everywhere! If a pioneer family wanted to have light, they made a fire in the fireplace and lit candles around the room. If a pioneer child needed to get up in the middle of the night, she might light a candle so she could see where to go. She had to be very careful with the candle. Why is important to be careful with candles?

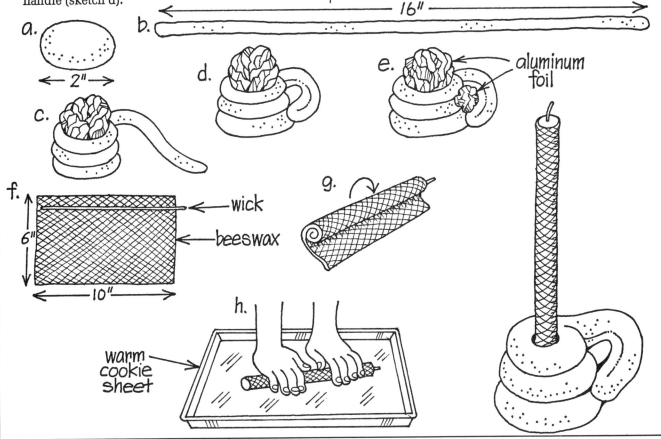

POM-POM BEE
(ONE-DAY PROJECT / 30 MINUTES)

Materials: Yellow and red felt, black chenille wire, black yarn, 2½-inch (6.25-cm) yellow pom-poms, 3/4-inch (1.9-cm) black pom-poms, 1/4-inch (.6-cm) wiggle eyes, scissors, ruler, pencils, glue, small plastic bags.

Preparation: Cut yarn into 10-inch (25-cm) lengths. Cut yellow felt into 4-inch (10-cm) squares. Cut red felt into 1-inch (2.5-cm) squares. For each child—fill a plastic bag with two yellow pom-poms, four black pom-poms, two wiggle eyes, one black chenille wire, one yellow felt square, a length of black yarn and a square of red felt.

Instruct each child in the following procedures:
- Cut two small pieces of black yarn for eyebrows. Cut mouth from red felt. Glue eyebrows, mouth and wiggle eyes to one yellow pom-pom to make a face (sketch a).
- Cut remaining black yarn in half. Glue each piece of yarn around second pom-pom (body) for stripes (sketch b).
- Glue black pom-poms to body for "hands" and "feet" (sketch b).
- Glue yellow pom-poms together (sketch c).
- Use pencil to draw two wings on yellow felt square and cut out (sketch d).
- Glue wings to back of bee.
- Cut chenille wire in half. Curl ends of wire and glue to bee's head for antennae.

Pioneer Life: A favorite activity of pioneer children was exploring. They took walks near their homes or wagon trains to see what they might find. Sometimes a pioneer child might discover a beehive while exploring. A beehive was an exciting find because it meant something sweet to eat—honey. It also meant "be careful" because bees can sting! Where do you like to explore?

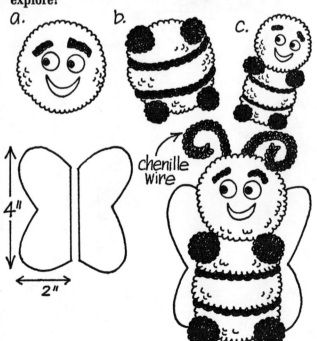

PIONEER FOLK
(ONE- OR TWO-DAY PROJECT / 60 MINUTES)

Materials: Pioneer Folk Clothes Patterns, tan or brown chenille wires, felt in various colors including tan or brown, felt pens, fabric scraps, yarn, glue, scissors, straight pins, photocopier and paper.

Preparation: Photocopy Clothes Patterns, one copy for each child.

Instruct each child in the following procedures:
- Twist one chenille wire to form a small loop for the head and a larger loop for the body (sketch a).
- Use scissors to cut another chenille wire in half.
- Twist one short chenille wire piece around neck to form arms (sketch b).
- Twist the other short chenille wire piece around bottom of body for legs (sketch b).
- Trace around chenille wire head onto tan or brown felt. Cut out circle and glue to head. Cut facial features, hair and hat from felt, fabric or yarn and glue in place.
- Pin Clothes Patterns to fabric and cut out clothes for Pioneer Folk. Glue onto chenille wire body.
- If time allows, children make additional Pioneer Folk.

Simplification Idea: Use felt pens to draw facial features.

Pioneer Life: What is one thing you do well? Pioneer people had to learn to do many things well. They had to make most of the things they needed. They made their own clothes, built their own homes and grew their own food. Even little children learned to help their parents make things. What is something you would like to learn how to do?

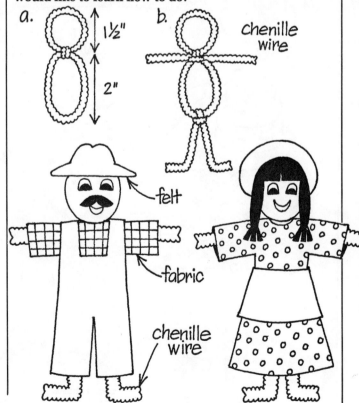

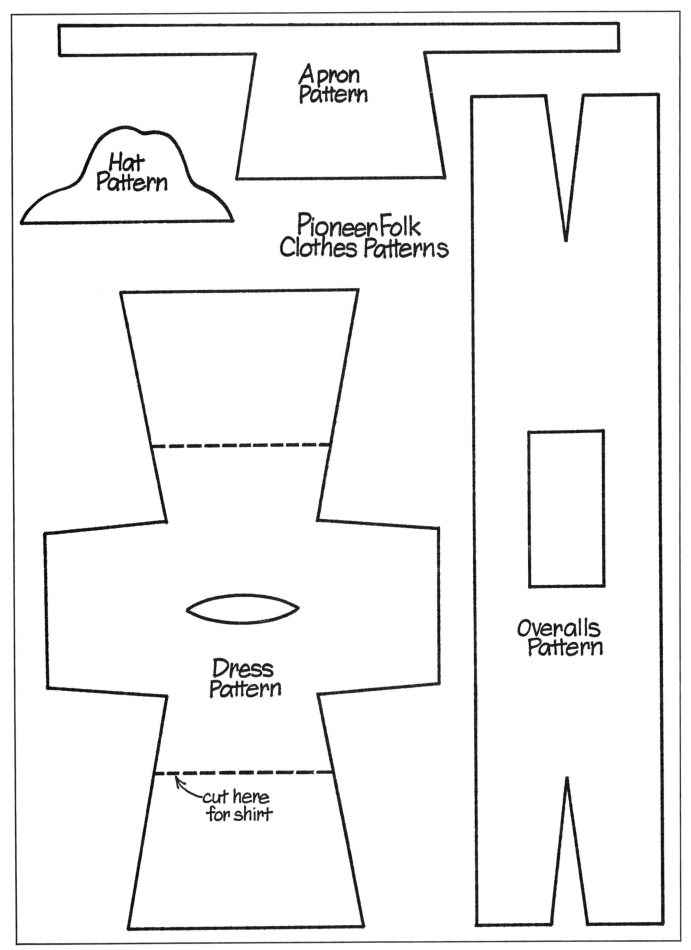

Apron
Pattern

Hat
Pattern

Pioneer Folk
Clothes Patterns

Dress
Pattern

cut here
for shirt

Overalls
Pattern

41

LOG CABIN
(TWO-DAY PROJECT / 30 MINUTES EACH DAY)

Materials: Log Cabin Side Pattern, bender board in 3³⁄₈-inch (8.4-cm) width, tagboard, plastic or paper drinking straws, scissors, felt pen, pencils, masking tape, glue, ruler, brown acrylic paint, paintbrushes, plastic paint containers, handsaw. Optional—fabric scraps.

Preparation: Trace Log Cabin Side Pattern onto tagboard and cut out. Label "Side." From tagboard cut a 6×8-inch (15×20-cm) rectangle and label "Front and Back." From additional tagboard cut an 8×10-inch (20×25-cm) rectangle and label "Roof."

Make a set of patterns for every three or four children. Cut bender board into 8-inch (20-cm) lengths— four for each child.

Instruct each child in the following procedures:
DAY ONE:
• Trace Log Cabin Patterns onto tagboard and cut out front, back, two sides and roof.
• Use scissors to cut out door and windows in front and side pieces of tagboard.
• Use tape to attach front and back to sides (sketch a).
• Fold roof and tape to cabin (sketch b).

• Use scissors to cut straws to fit walls around doors and windows. Glue straws to cover front, back and sides of cabin (see sketch). Let dry.
DAY TWO:
• Glue two overlapping pieces of bender board to each side of roof (see sketch). Hold in place while glue dries.
• Paint straws and triangular sides of roof with brown paint.

Enrichment Idea: Cut fabric scraps and glue inside windows for curtains.

Pioneer Life: **What do you like about the place you live? When the pioneers reached their destination they couldn't just rent a house or an apartment. There were no ready-made houses on the prairie—only miles and miles of land. The pioneers had to build their own homes. Sometimes all the people around pitched in to help a new family build a log cabin. They cut down trees and used the logs to build a home in just a few days. Let's pretend a nearby yard or field is a prairie. What spot would you choose to build your log cabin? Why would you choose that spot?**

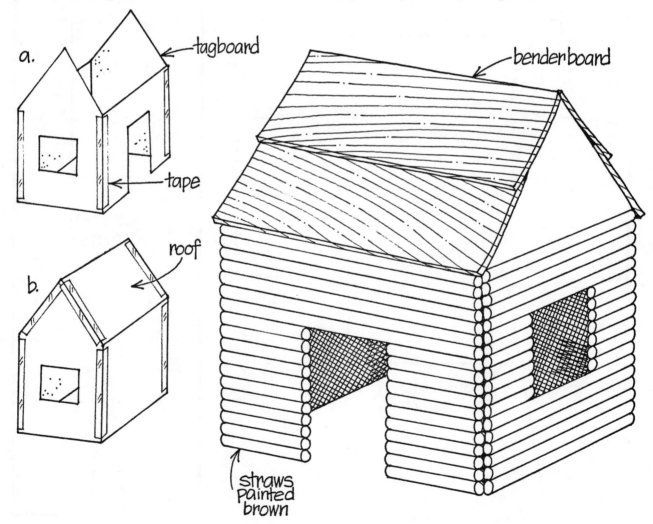

a. tagboard

tape

roof

b.

benderboard

straws painted brown

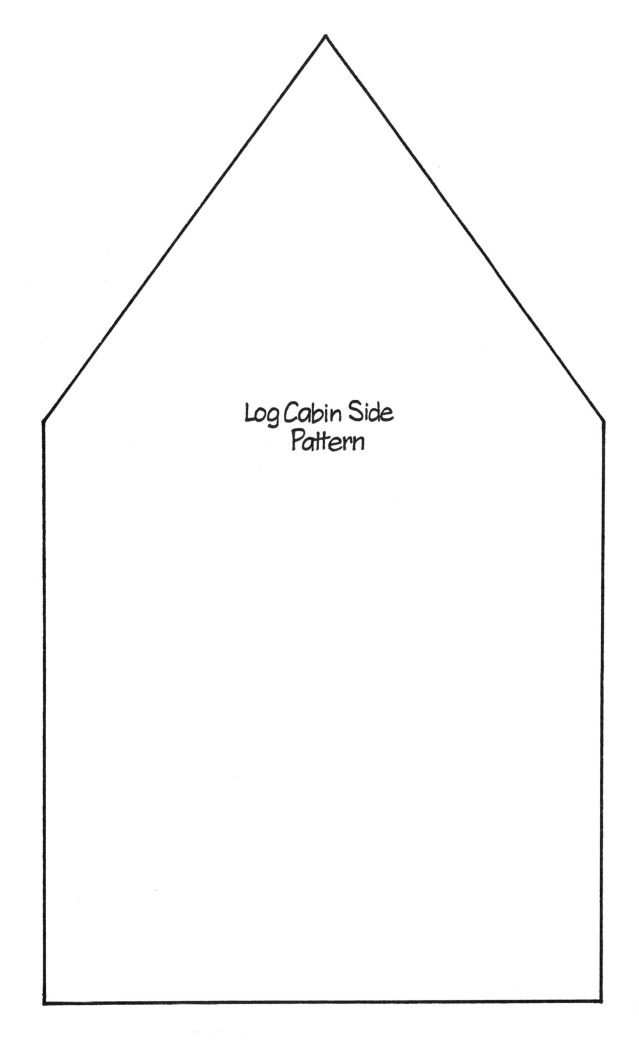

Log Cabin Side
Pattern

43

WATER WELL
(TWO-DAY PROJECT / 30 MINUTES EACH DAY)

Materials: Well Roof Pattern, tagboard, 1/4-inch (.6-cm) diameter wooden dowels, 1/2-inch (1.25-cm) wide balsa wood, yarn or cord, white butcher paper, glue, pencil, felt markers or crayons, scissors, ruler, masking tape, hole punch, handsaw. For each child—oatmeal container, small plastic cup, 26 wooden craft sticks. Optional—one small margarine tub for each child.

Preparation: Trace Well Roof Pattern onto tagboard and cut out. Make a pattern for every three or four children.

Cut oatmeal containers so they are 5 inches (12.5 cm) high—one for each child. Cut white paper into 5×18-inch (12.5×45-cm) sheets—one for each child. Cut dowels into 9-inch (22.5-cm) lengths—one for each child. Cut balsa wood into 9-inch (22.5-cm) lengths—two for each child. Cut yarn or cord into 14-inch (35-cm) lengths—one for each child.

Instruct each child in the following procedures:
DAY ONE:
- Glue balsa wood lengths inside oatmeal container (sketch a).
- Trace Well Roof Pattern onto tagboard twice and cut out.
- Tape roof pieces together at top (sketch b). Fold sides of roof and tape in place (sketch c).
- Use hole punch to punch one hole in center of each triangular side of roof (sketch d).
- Glue craft sticks to slanted sides of roof (sketch d).

- Lay well on its side and glue balsa wood to inside of roof just below holes (sketch e.) Let dry.
DAY TWO:
- Use felt pens and/or crayons to draw stones on sheet of white paper.
- Glue paper sheet to cover outside of oatmeal container.
- Tie cord to center of dowel and secure with glue (sketch f). Let dry.
- Use hole punch to punch holes on opposite sides of plastic cup near the rim. Thread end of cord through holes and tie a knot (sketch f).
- From inside of roof, place ends of dowel through holes in roof.
- Turn dowel to cause "bucket" to go up or down.

Enrichment Idea: Lay sheet of butcher paper on a rough surface such as a sidewalk while using crayon to draw stones. The surface of the sidewalk will create a textured effect. Also, children may want to place margarine tubs full of water inside their wells and actually draw out water with their buckets.

Pioneer Life: **Where does your water come from? Pioneers didn't have running water in their homes. If they didn't live near a river they had to dig a very deep hole until they found water. That is called a well. Anyone who needed water lowered a bucket into the well and got fresh, cool water. Put a container of water in your well and draw up some water in your bucket. How does your well work?**

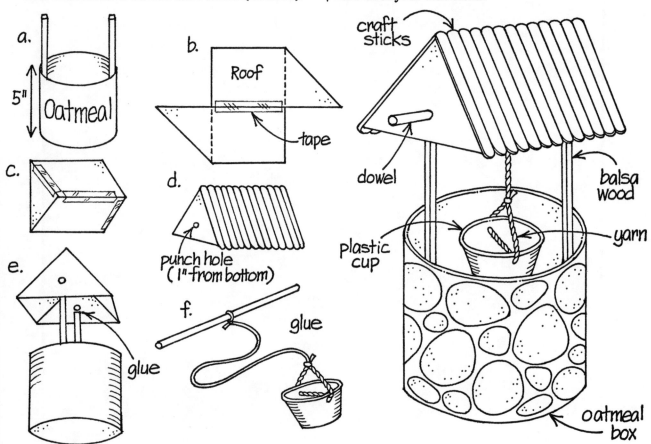

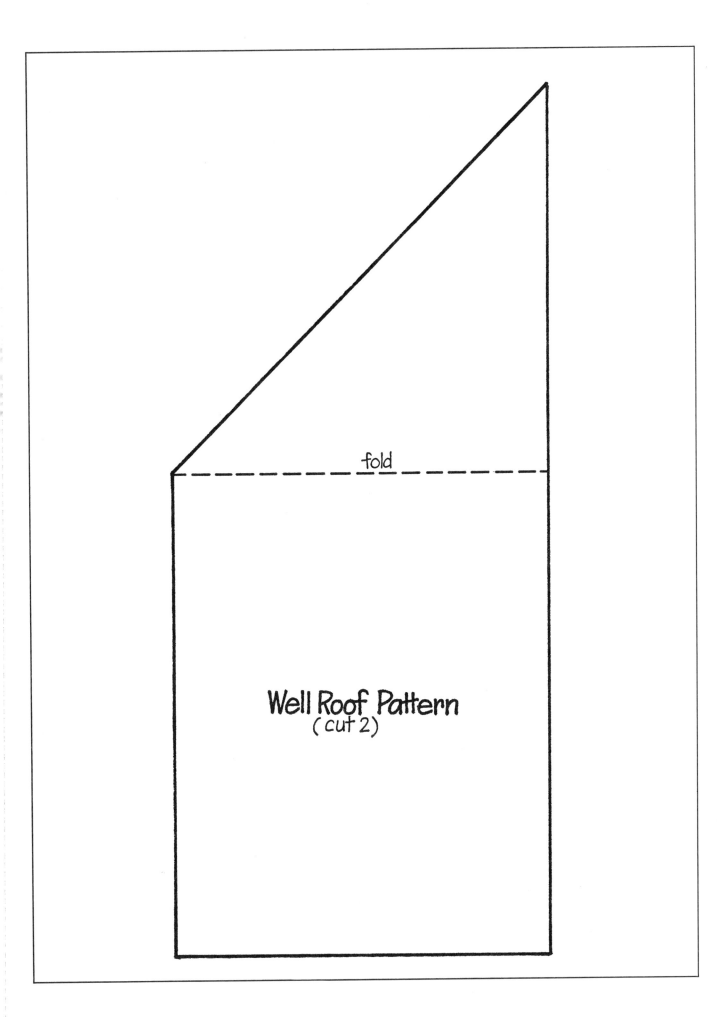

fold

Well Roof Pattern
(cut 2)

APPLIQUÉD QUILT SQUARE
(ONE-DAY PROJECT / 30 MINUTES)

Note: If you wish to use these squares to make a quilt, see page 7 for quilt instructions. If you are not making a quilt, follow instructions below to make bandanas from individual squares. The Bandana is a two-day project—30 minutes each day.

Materials: Muslin, 100% cotton fabric scraps (solid colors and calicos), tubes of dimensional fabric paint in several colors (available at fabric or craft supply stores), lightweight fusible interfacing with peel-off backing such as "Wonder Under," pressing cloth, iron, ironing board, scissors, measuring tape, pencils, white paper. To make bandanas—sewing machine, thread, straight pins, sewing needles, solid color fabric.

Preparation: Wash and dry all fabric to preshrink. Cut muslin into 9-inch (22.5-cm) squares—one for each student. Cut interfacing to size of fabric scraps and iron to fuse together. To make scarves—on the bias, cut a triangular shape of coordinating fabric 37×26×26 inches (92.5×63×63-cm)—one for each student (sketch a). Use sewing machine to hem longer edge of each scarf.

Instruct each student in the following procedures:
- Draw a simple design on white paper.
- Copy design onto fabric scraps (fused with interfacing) and cut out.
- Peel paper backing off cut design pieces. Position design pieces on muslin square with fabric side up (sketch b). Allow at least a 1/2-inch (1.25-cm) border around edges of square.
- Use iron to fuse design pieces onto muslin square.
- Trace around all design pieces with dimensional paints. Let dry.

If you are making a quilt, see page 7. If students are making bandanas, they follow these procedures:
- Unravel four or five threads along the shorter edges of bandana (sketch c).
- Teacher turns edges of muslin square under 1/4 inch (.6-cm) and irons. (Be sure not to touch fabric paint to hot iron.)
- Position quilt square on right side of bandana and pin in place.
- Use needle and thread to stitch square to bandana. Tack center of appliqué square to scarf by stitching inside the design.

Enrichment Idea: Students use Quilt Square Designs (page 9) to get ideas for their appliqué designs.

Pioneer Life: **How does your family remember special events?** (Photo albums, scrap books, video tapes, souvenirs.) **Pioneer women sometimes designed quilts that told about their families. For instance, they might embroider the names of each family member, when they were born, where they lived, who they married and when they died.**

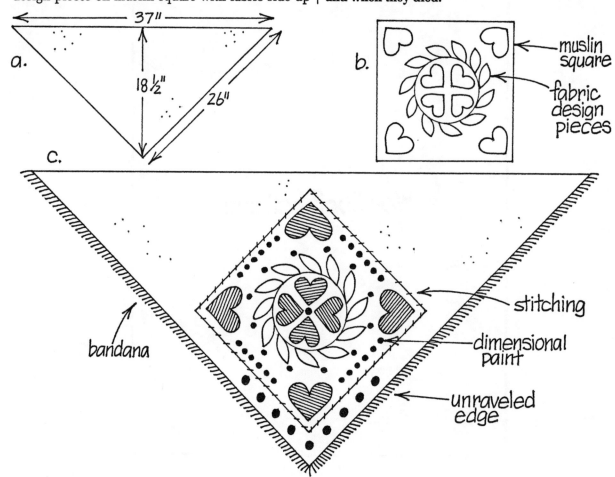

a. 37" 18½" 26"

b. muslin square / fabric design pieces

c. bandana / stitching / dimensional paint / unraveled edge

PEG RACK

(TWO-DAY PROJECT / 30 MINUTES EACH DAY)

Materials: White paper, pencils, 1×6-inch (2.5×15-cm) pine board, 1/2-inch (1.25-cm) diameter wood dowels, drill with 1/2-inch (1.25-cm) bit, fine-tooth saw, sandpaper, hammer, ruler, craft knife, acrylic paints in bright, intense colors, paintbrushes, newspapers, white glue, damp paper towels, clear acrylic spray. For each student—one picture hanger and small nail.

Preparation: Cut pine board into 16-inch (40-cm) lengths—one for each student. Cut dowels into 2½-inch (6.25-cm) lengths—four for each student. On each board, mark position of peg holes (sketch a). Using 1/2-inch (1.25-cm) drill bit, drill 1/2-inch (1.25-cm) deep peg holes on each board.

Instruct each student in the following procedures:
DAY ONE:
• In a well ventilated area, cover work surface with newspapers.
• Use sandpaper to sand four pegs and front side of pine board until smooth.
• Draw design for rack on white paper. Then copy design onto rack.
• Paint design on board.
• Squeeze several drops of glue into each peg hole. Insert dowels. Use a damp paper towel to wipe off any excess glue. Allow to dry overnight.
DAY TWO:
• Nail picture hanger to center back, 1 inch (2.5-cm) from the top.
• In well ventilated area, spray assembled stenciled peg rack with clear acrylic spray. Allow to dry. Spray with second coat.

Enrichment Idea: Make stencils using patterns on page 10. Students paint stencil designs on Peg Rack.

Pioneer Life: **What does the inside of your closet look like? Is it messy? Most pioneers didn't have dressers or closets. They placed their dishes on shelves or crates and hung their clothes on pegs much like the peg rack you've made.**

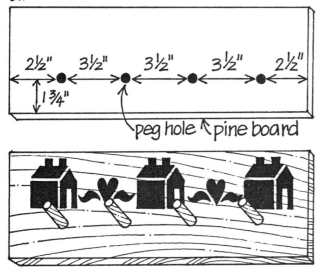

a.

2½" 3½" 3½" 3½" 2½"

1¾"

peg hole pine board

SWIRLED WATER CANDLE

(ONE-DAY PROJECT / 30 MINUTES)

Materials: Paraffin (approximately three cakes for each student), various colors of broken crayons, vegetable oil, double boiler, coffee cans, pot holders, stove, rubber gloves, buckets, water, paper towels. For each student—one 6×1½-inch (15×3.75-cm) candle, one small mixing bowl with smooth sides 5-6 inches (12.5-15 cm) deep.

Preparation: Place paraffin in coffee can. Place coffee can in double boiler and heat to melt paraffin. Drop in one color of broken crayons until desired color is achieved. Fill bucket with lukewarm water and surround with towels or place outside.

Instruct each student in the following procedures:
• Use paper towel to generously oil inside of mixing bowl.
• Place candle in center of bowl.
• With teacher's help, pour 1/2 inch (1.25-cm) of hot wax into bowl to anchor candle. Let wax cool and harden (sketch a).
• With teacher's help, pour 2 inches (5-cm) hot wax into bowl.
• Put on rubber gloves. Grasp the bowl with two hands. Plunge bowl and candle into water-filled bucket, turning the bowl as it submerges (sketch b). Turning the bowl causes the hot wax to spiral around the candle.
• When wax has hardened and cooled, invert bowl, tap lightly and the candle should release. If it doesn't release, heat a pan of water and quickly dip base of bowl into water. Immediately lift candle from bowl.

Enrichment Idea: With teacher's supervision, students complete the preparation for the craft.

Pioneer Life: **Has the electricity in your house ever gone off at night? What did you do?** (Allow students to answer.) **Pioneers had no electric lights. Whenever they needed light they made a fire or lit candles or lanterns. Pioneers often made the candles their families needed and sometimes sold any extra candles to make money.**

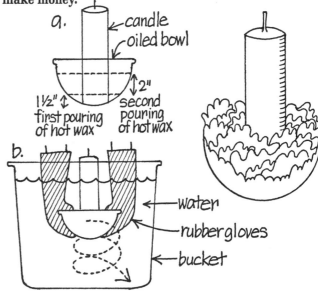

a. candle
oiled bowl

1½" 2"
first pouring second
of hot wax pouring
of hot wax

b.

water

rubber gloves

bucket

RAG TRIVET

(ONE- OR TWO-DAY PROJECT / 60 MINUTES)

Materials: Basket coiling in 1/2-inch (1.25-cm) diameter (available at fabric and craft supply stores), scissors, ruler, tape. For each child—one large plastic needle (available at fabric or craft supply stores), 1/2-yard (45-cm) of 45-inch (1.12-m) wide colorful, cotton fabric.

Preparation: Cut basket coiling into 6-foot (1.8-m) lengths—one for each child. Use scissors to angle ends of coiling (sketch a). Tear fabric into 1½-inch (3.75-cm) wide strips.

Instruct each child in the following procedures:

- Wrap tape around each end of coil to secure.
- Use tape to attach fabric strip to coil about 5 inches (12.5-cm) from end (sketch b).
- Wrap fabric around coil to the end (sketch c). As you wind, overlap fabric so coil does not show through.
- Thread fabric strip through eye of needle (sketch c).
- Wind fabric-covered section of coil into a spiral (sketch d).
- Secure spiral in place by wrapping fabric strip once around outside of spiral and once through center of spiral (sketches e and f).
- Wrap next section of coil with fabric several times (sketch g).
- Wind covered coil around spiral and attach by threading fabric strip once around outside of spiral and once through adjoining coil (sketch h).
- Continue this process of wrapping coil with fabric and winding coil. Secure every few inches by wrapping fabric once around adjoining coil.
- When you come to the end of a strip of fabric, tape end onto coil. Begin again with a new fabric strip, taping it in place and winding fabric to cover tape.
- To complete trivet, wrap fabric to end of coil and secure by threading fabric over adjoining coil. Then thread fabric under several wraps of fabric. Cut off any extra fabric (sketch i).

Enrichment Idea: Have children tear their own fabric strips.

Pioneer Life: **What do most people do with a pile of rags? Throw them away? In pioneer times people didn't throw things away so quickly. They used whatever they had to make things they needed. Rags could be used to make warm quilts for their beds, colorful baskets, thick rugs, or trivets like you've made today. What do you throw away that could be used to make something else?**

RAG BASKET

(ONE- OR TWO-DAY PROJECT / 60 MINUTES)

Materials: Basket coiling in 1/4-inch (.6-cm) diameter (available at fabric and craft supply stores), scissors, pencil, ruler, transparent tape. For each student—one large plastic needle (available at fabric and craft supply stores), 1/3 yard (30-cm) of 45-inch (112.5-cm) solid color cotton fabric, 1/3 yard of 45-inch (112.5-cm) coordinating cotton print fabric.

Preparation: Cut basket coiling into 8-foot (2.4-m) lengths—one for each student. Use scissors to angle ends of coiling (sketch a). Wrap ends with tape to keep from raveling. Tear fabric into 1½-inch (3.75-cm) wide strips.

Instruct each student in the following procedures:

- Choose a solid color fabric strip and tape one end to coil about 5 inches (12.5-cm) from the tapered end (sketch b).
- Spiraling toward the tapered end, tightly wrap fabric strip around coil. As you wind, overlap fabric so coil does not show through (sketch c).
- Thread loose end of fabric strip through eye of needle (sketch c).
- Wind fabric-covered section of coil into a tight, flat spiral (sketch d).
- Secure spiral by tightly wrapping fabric strip once around outside coil of spiral and once through center of spiral (sketches e and f).
- Wrap fabric strip around uncovered coil three or four times (sketch g). Then wrap covered coil around spiral. Secure outer coil to adjoining spiral coil by threading fabric strip around both coils (sketch h).
- Wrap and secure coil in this manner until there are six rows in the spiral, forming a base about 4 inches (10-cm) across. (When you come to the end of a fabric strip, tape end onto coil. Begin again with a new fabric strip, taping it in place and winding fabric to cover tape.)
- Shape basket sides by winding coils to rest on top of spiral base. Continue attaching top coil to adjoining bottom coil as you spiral sides upward (sketch j). Continue using solid color fabric for the first three rows, then change to coordinating print fabric. Make eight rows using print fabric.
- Use solid color fabric strips to make the two final rows.
- To make basket handle: Wrap next 10 inches (25-cm) of coil with solid color fabric. Arch wrapped coil across top of basket (see sketch of completed basket). Secure end of handle by wrapping fabric through adjoining lower coil and around handle.
- To complete basket, cut off extra coil at an angle. Wrap the fabric to end of coil and secure by threading fabric over adjoining coil. Then thread the fabric back under several wraps of fabric. Cut off any extra fabric.

Enrichment Idea: Have students tear their own strips of fabric.

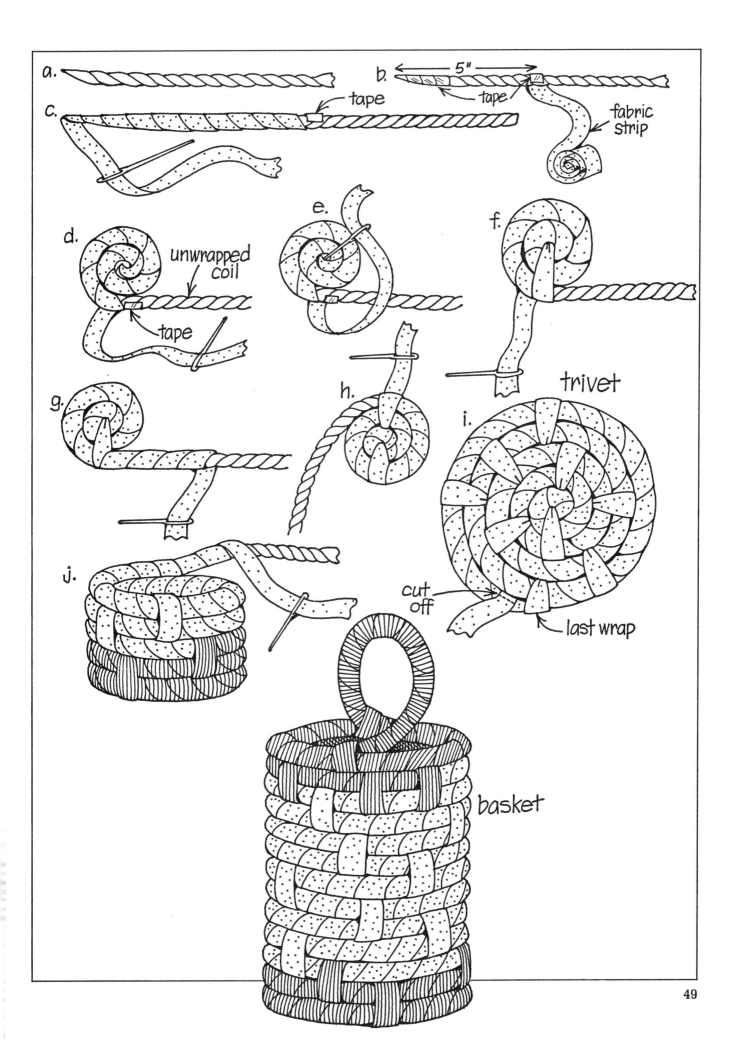

a.

b. 5"

tape

c. tape

fabric strip

d. unwrapped coil

tape

e.

f.

trivet

g.

h.

i.

cut off

last wrap

j.

basket

GRASS HORSE
(ONE-DAY PROJECT / 30 MINUTES)

Materials: Wild grass 36 inches (90-cm) or more in length (picked from a field), green or brown yarn, ruler, scissors, 1/16-inch (.15-cm) diameter dowels, craft knife, string, fine-toothed saw, buckets, water.

Preparation: Cut yarn into 60-inch (150-cm) lengths—four for each student. Cut dowels into 4-inch (10-cm) lengths, one for each student. Cut off grass heads (tassles) and save. Use string to tie 10-blade bundles of grass—three for each student (sketch a). Soak bundles in a bucket of water for one hour before use. Shake off excess water.

Instruct each student in the following procedures:

- Tap first bundle of grass on a flat surface so ends are even at one end. Bend bundle in three places to form head, neck and body (sketch b). Neck should be approximately 4 inches (10-cm) long.
- Wrap a length of yarn around horse's nose several times and knot. Then move yarn to next wrapping point and repeat process (sketch c). After you have wrapped yarn in all designated places, knot yarn and cut off excess.
- Bend second bundle in thirds to form two legs and body (sketch d). Body section should be the same length as body section of first bundle. Firmly wrap yarn around bundle at intervals, knotting as you go (sketch d). Trim excess yarn.
- Repeat prior step with third bundle.
- Assemble the three bundles together, firmly wrapping and knotting yarn at each end of body (sketch e). Trim excess yarn. Trim legs so they are of equal length and appropriate size for horse.
- Carefully insert dowel up through grass that makes up chest, neck and forehead. This will add strength to neck and help keep head upright.
- For mane and tail, insert grass heads into bundles (sketch f).

Enrichment Idea: Students fashion bridle and reins using colorful yarn, and a saddle using leaves or felt. Attach saddle to horse using a needle and thread.

Pioneer Life: **Have you ever gone horseback riding? Did you enjoy it? Pioneers often rode horses, for work, transportation and pleasure.**

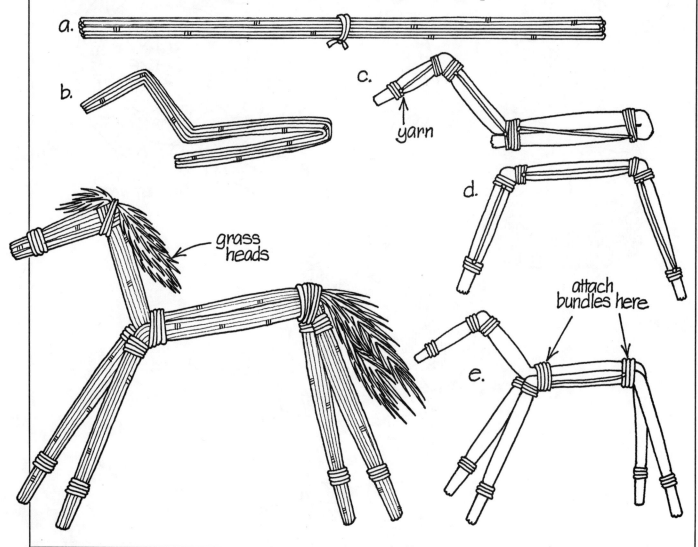

a.

b.

c.
yarn

d.

grass heads

attach bundles here

e.

PIONEER LIFE DIORAMA

The following pages contain instructions for making a Pioneer Diorama. Have your students begin by making the Background Scene. Then choose one or more of the other options, depending on the time and materials available, to complete the Diorama.

PIONEER LIFE DIORAMA—BACKGROUND SCENE
(ONE-DAY PROJECT / 30 MINUTES)

Materials: Craft knife, pencils, rulers, tempera paints, shallow containers for paint, paintbrushes, sponges, tacky glue, air-drying clay, miscellaneous nature items (small rocks, leaves, twigs, pine needles, grass clippings, foliage). For each student—one cardboard box, approximately 9×12×18 inches (22.5×30×45-cm).

Preparation: Use craft knife to cut off top flaps and front of each box. Leave a 1-inch (2.5-cm) lip on bottom front of each box. Cut sponges into 2-inch (5-cm) squares. Pour paint into containers.

Instruct each student in the following procedures:
- Use a pencil to draw a backdrop of hills and sky on the inside of the box. Paint with appropriate colors.
- To create clouds, sponge white paint in sky. Sponge several shades of brown paint onto the inside bottom of box to create the mottled effect of dirt. Let dry.

To complete Diorama (after optional items have been made):
- Arrange items in the Background Scene and glue in place.
- Add small rocks, leaves, twigs, pine needles, grass clippings and foliage to the scene. Glue in place.
- For trees, press ends of foliage into clay bases. Prop up while drying and then glue in place.

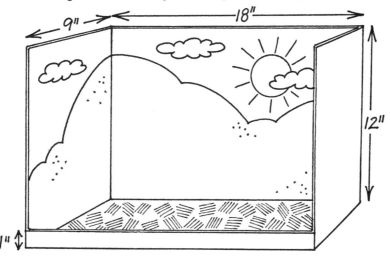

PIONEER LIFE DIORAMA—CLOTHESPIN PIONEERS
(ONE- OR TWO-DAY PROJECT / 60 MINUTES)

Materials: Clothespin Pioneers Clothes Patterns, straight pins, yarn for hair, thread to match yarn, tan chenille wires, scissors, ruler, tacky glue, calico and gingham fabric scraps (tiny patterns will work best), tan or brown felt, air-drying clay, 1/8-inch (.3-cm) ribbon, photocopier and paper. For each student—two 3³/₄-inch (9.4-cm) wooden clothespins with rounded tops.

Preparation: Photocopy Clothes Patterns—one for each student. Cut chenille wires into 4¹/₄-inch (10.6-cm) lengths—two for each student. Cut ribbon into 4-inch (10-cm) lengths—two for each student. Cut yarn into 30-inch (75-cm) lengths—two for each student.

Instruct each student in the following procedures:
TO MAKE PIONEER WOMAN:
- Cut apart Clothes Patterns. Pin dress, apron and scarf patterns to fabric scraps and cut out.
- Slip clothespin head through opening in center of fabric dress. Lift front of dress up. Wrap back of dress around front and glue (sketch a).
- Bend ends of chenille wire to form hands. Lay chenille wire across neck and arms of dress (sketch a).
- Fold front of dress down and around to the back and glue (sketch b). Glue sleeves as shown in sketch b.
- Fold Apron and Scarf on fold lines. Thread ribbon through apron and scarf at folds. Wrap scarf around doll's neck and tie with a knot. Wrap apron around waist and tie with a knot.
- Wrap yarn for hair loosely around three fingers seven times (sketch c). Slip yarn off fingers. Use matching thread to tie looped yarn in two places. Cut loops, trim bangs and ponytail (sketch d). Glue hair onto

head of clothespin.
- To make a stand, press bottom of clothespin into a small ball of clay. Let dry.

TO MAKE PIONEER MAN:
- Pin Buckskin Shirt and Pant Leg Patterns to felt and cut out. Cut fringe on shirt as indicated on pattern. Fold shirt in half along fold line.
- Pin Bandana Pattern to fabric and cut out.
- Wrap Pant Leg around doll's leg and glue (sketch e). Repeat with other Pant Leg.
- Slip head through opening in center of shirt.
- Bend ends of chenille wire to form hands. Lay chenille wire across neck and arms of shirt (sketch a). Glue shirt together under arms and along sides.
- Center the point of bandana on doll's back. Wrap ends around neck and cross over chest. Secure with glue.
- Wrap yarn for hair loosely around three fingers seven times (sketch c). Slip yarn off fingers. Use matching thread to tie looped yarn in two places. Cut loops, trim bangs and ponytail (sketch d). Glue hair on head of clothespin.
- Press bottom of clothespin into a small ball of clay. Allow to dry.

Pioneer Life: **What chores do you do at home? Pioneers had many chores to do every day. The men built log cabins and barns. They hunted, chopped wood for fires, planted crops and tended animals. Women worked in the garden, cooked, sewed, and cleaned. They even made their own soap and candles. Would you rather do your chores or the chores of a pioneer?**

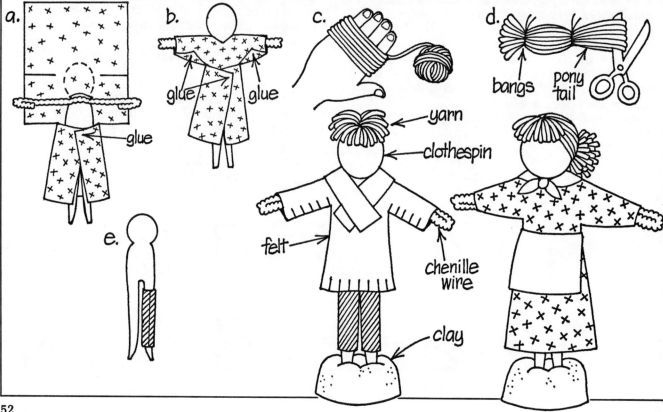

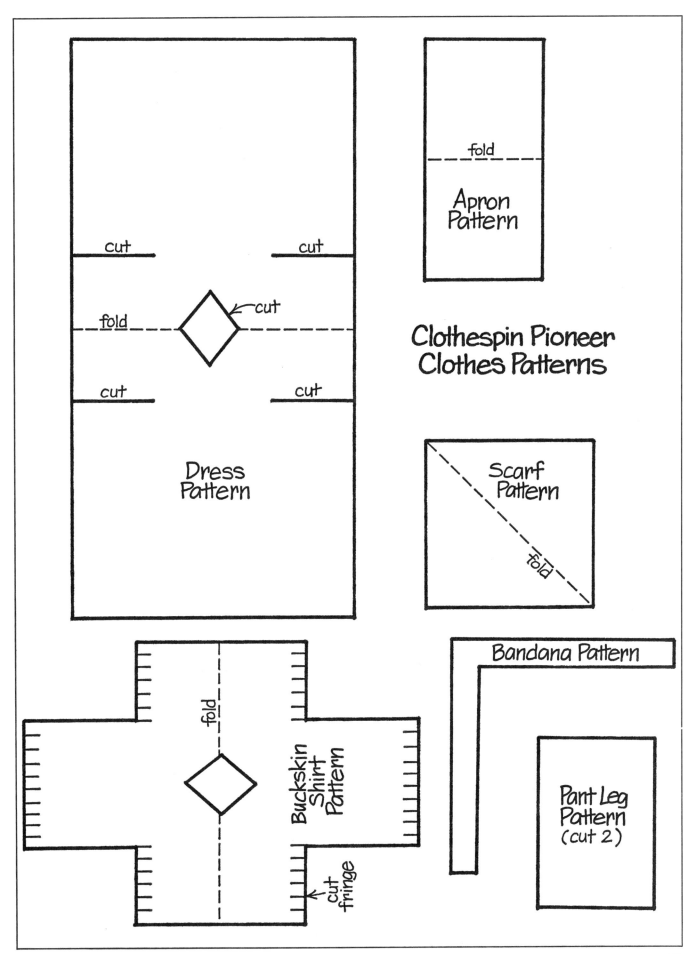

cut   cut

cut

fold

cut   cut

Dress
Pattern

fold

Apron
Pattern

Clothespin Pioneer
Clothes Patterns

Scarf
Pattern

fold

fold

Buckskin
Shirt
Pattern

cut
fringe

Bandana Pattern

Pant Leg
Pattern
(cut 2)

53

PIONEER LIFE DIORAMA—LOG CABIN
(ONE- OR TWO-DAY PROJECT / 60 MINUTES)

Materials: Tacky glue, dark brown poster board, heavy-duty shears, masking tape, scissors, pencil, ruler, craft knife, plastic bags. For each student—150 wooden craft sticks. Optional: Medium and dark brown construction paper.

Preparation: Use shears to cut craft sticks into 1/2-inch (1.25-cm) lengths—45 for each student. (These will be spacers.) Cut additional craft sticks into 1¼-inch (3.1-cm) lengths—18 for each student. (These will be used to make window jambs.) Finally, cut additional craft sticks into 1½-inch (3.75-cm) lengths—16 for each student. (These will be used to make the right door jamb.)

Use craft knife to cut poster board into 9×8-inch (22.5×20-cm) Roof Top pieces—one for each student. Cut additional poster board into 1½×½-inch (3.75×1.25-cm) Shutter pieces—two for each student. Cut additional poster board into 4½x3½x3½-inch (11.25x8.75x8.75-cm) triangles for Side Roof pieces —two for each student.

Place 90 craft sticks, 45 wood spacers, 18 window pieces, 16 door pieces, two Side Roof pieces, two Roof Top pieces and two Shutters in each plastic bag—one bag for each student.

Instruct each student in the following procedures:
• Sort wood pieces into piles according to size.
• Overlap and glue six full-size sticks together as in sketch a. This will be the base of your cabin.

• Stack and glue sticks to raise the walls (sketch b). Back and side walls use full-size sticks and will be 19 or 20 sticks high. Front wall will use window pieces, door pieces and spacers (sketch b). Door opening will be 16 sticks and 17 spacers high. Window opening will be nine sticks and nine spacers high. Wall above window and door will be three sticks high.
• Fold Roof Top pieces in half.
• Tape Roof Top to Side Roof pieces, leaving a 1/2-inch (1.25-cm) overhang (sketch c).
• Place a drop of glue on each corner of the house and set roof on top of house. Let dry.
• Glue shutters to the sides of the windows.

Enrichment Idea: Cut medium and dark brown construction paper into 1¼×¾-inch (3.1×1.9-cm) rectangular shapes. Starting at the bottom edge of the roof and working in horizontal rows, glue on construction paper "shingles." Randomly place the two shades of brown "shingles" and completely cover surface of roof.

Pioneer Life: **How well do you know your neighbors? Have they ever helped you? Have you ever helped them? When a pioneer family reached their destination they built their own home. Often their neighbors pitched in to help the new family build a log cabin or raise a barn. They cut down trees and used the logs to build a home in just a few days.**

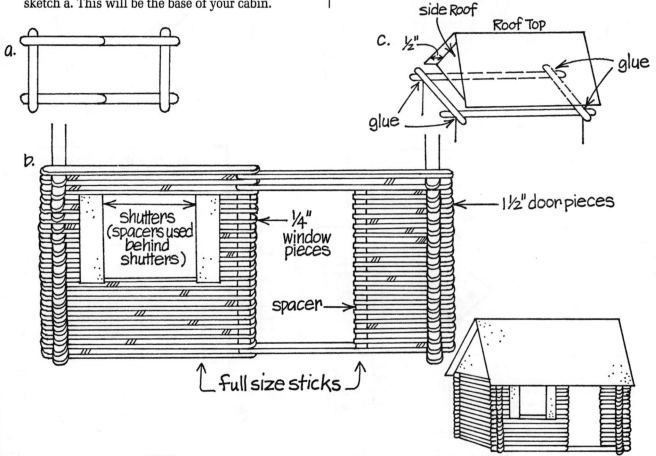

PIONEER LIFE DIORAMA SALT CLAY ANIMALS

(TWO-DAY PROJECT / 60 MINUTES)

Materials: Salt, flour, water, large mixing bowl, measuring cup, plastic bag, tempera paint, paintbrushes, shallow pans for paint.

Preparation: For every two students—mix one cup flour with one cup salt in large mixing bowl. Add a little cool water and mix with hands. If mixture is too dry, add a little more water. Mix with hands until you have a ball of clay that is firm but not sticky. If sticky, add more flour. Store in plastic bag until ready to use. On second day, pour paint into containers.

Instruct each student in the following procedures:
DAY ONE:
- Use clay to shape animals in keeping with the overall size of diorama.
- Let clay dry overnight. (Optional: Accelerate drying time by placing animals on a baking sheet in a slightly warm oven.)

DAY TWO:
- Paint animals.

Pioneer Life: **What kind of pet do you have? What do you do to take care of your (dog)? Pioneers had many animals. Sometimes they raised chickens and pigs for food. They often kept horses or oxen to pull wagons and plows. Pioneers also had dogs and cats as pets, just like we do today.**

PIONEER LIFE DIORAMA QUERN

(TWO-DAY PROJECT / 30 MINUTES)

Materials: Air-drying clay, twigs, knife, tempera paint, paintbrushes, drinking glasses, plastic containers for paint.

Preparation: On second day, pour paint into the containers.

Instruct each student in the following procedures:
DAY ONE:
- Flatten a piece of clay to 3/8-inch (.9-cm).
- Use glass to cut two round shapes from the flattened clay.
- Set one of the circles aside to dry. Use knife to cut a small funnel-shaped hole in the center of the second circle. Insert a twig into the side edge for a handle. Allow to dry.

DAY TWO:
- Paint both circles. Let dry.
- Place circle with handle (top stone) on top of other circle (bottom stone).

Pioneer Life: **A quern was used by pioneers to grind corn kernels into meal or flour. This meal was then used for baking bread. The quern was made from two flat, circular stones. The lower stone was fastened in the ground so it wouldn't move. After pouring corn kernels through an opening in the top stone, a pioneer grasped the handle and turned the top stone to grind the kernels into meal.**

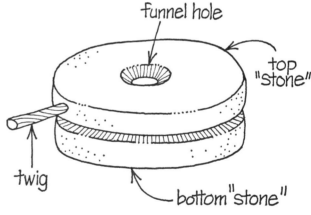

funnel hole

top "stone"

twig

bottom "stone"

PIONEER LIFE DIORAMA WORM FENCE

(ONE-DAY PROJECT / 30 MINUTES)

Materials: Paper drinking straws, rulers, pencils, scissors, glue, brown tempera paint, paintbrushes, plastic containers, newspapers.

Preparation: Cover work area with newspapers. Pour paint into plastic containers.

Instruct each student in the following procedures:

• Mark straws in 2½-inch (6.25-cm) increments and cut.

• Place two straw pieces (logs) in a "V" shape and glue crossed ends (sketch a).

• Glue on additional straw pieces to make fence as long as is desired (sketch b).

• Add a row of logs on top of the first row, gluing the ends of each log in place. Continue building in this way until the fence is as high as desired (sketch c). Let dry.

• Paint fence and let dry.

Pioneer Life: **Early settlers made log fences that looked much like the fences you're making. They were called worm fences because they seemed to wiggle like a worm all over the countryside.**

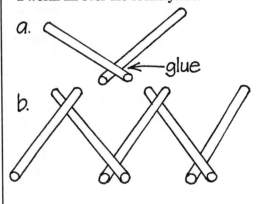

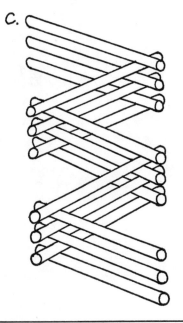

PIONEER LIFE DIORAMA WELL AND SWEEP

(ONE-DAY PROJECT / 30 MINUTES)

Materials: Air-drying clay, gravel or small pebbles, chenille wire, string, ruler, scissors, aluminum foil. For each student—one 2½-ounce baby food jar, one thin stick about 4½ inches long that is crotched close to one end (see sketch), one thin stick about 8 inches long.

Preparation: Wash baby food jars and discard metal lids. Cut chenille wire into 1½-inch (3.75-cm) lengths —one for each student. Cut aluminum foil into 5-inch (12.5-cm) squares—one for each student. Cut string into 4-inch (10-cm) lengths—one for each student.

Instruct each student in the following procedures:

FOR WELL:

• Cover outside of baby food jar with clay. Press pebbles into surface of clay, leaving ridges of clay between pebbles. Let dry.

FOR SWEEP:

• Push the straight end of crotched stick into a ball of clay to make a base. Let dry.

• Wrap chenille wire twice around one end of the longer stick. Shape the loose end of the wire into a hook.

FOR BUCKET:

• Crimp square of foil into the shape of a bucket in keeping with dimensions of your well. With the end of the scissors, poke a small hole on either side of the bucket. Thread string through holes and tie to form a handle. Trim off excess string.

• Lay long, sweep stick across crotched stick so hook hangs over the well. Hang bucket on hook.

Pioneer Life: **What do you use water for during a typical day? Pioneers needed water for drinking, washing, cooking and watering their crops, but they didn't have water pipes and faucets like we do. They dug deep holes in the ground until they found water. Then they built some sort of wall around the well to keep dirt from falling in. Anyone who needed water could lower a bucket into the well and draw up fresh, cool water.**

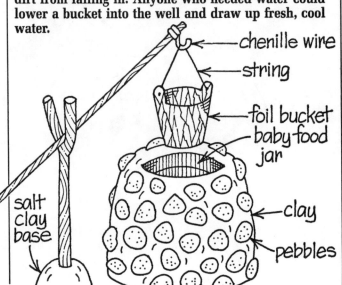

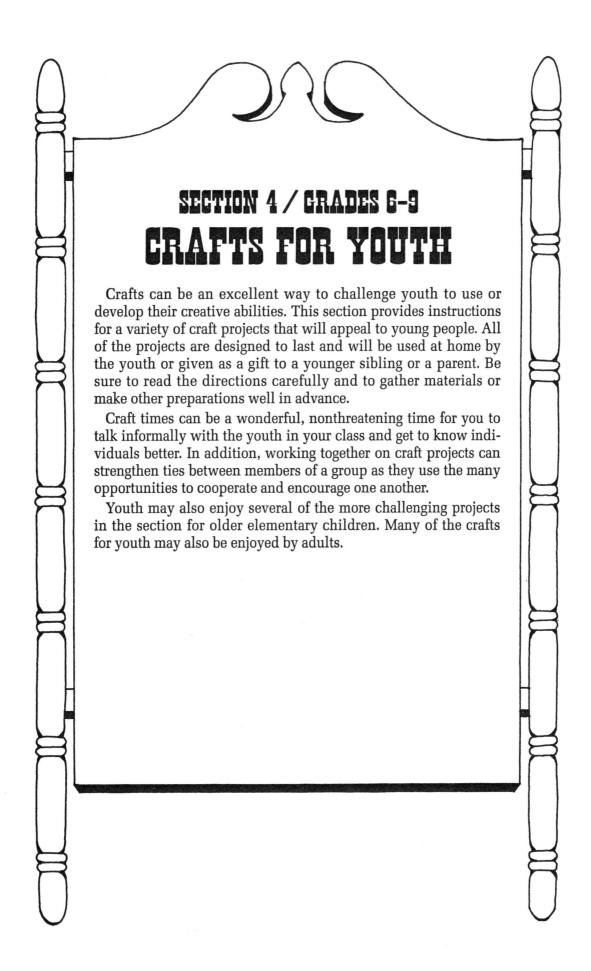

SECTION 4 / GRADES 6-9
CRAFTS FOR YOUTH

Crafts can be an excellent way to challenge youth to use or develop their creative abilities. This section provides instructions for a variety of craft projects that will appeal to young people. All of the projects are designed to last and will be used at home by the youth or given as a gift to a younger sibling or a parent. Be sure to read the directions carefully and to gather materials or make other preparations well in advance.

Craft times can be a wonderful, nonthreatening time for you to talk informally with the youth in your class and get to know individuals better. In addition, working together on craft projects can strengthen ties between members of a group as they use the many opportunities to cooperate and encourage one another.

Youth may also enjoy several of the more challenging projects in the section for older elementary children. Many of the crafts for youth may also be enjoyed by adults.

BATIK QUILT SQUARE
(ONE-DAY PROJECT / 30 MINUTES)

Note: If you wish to use these squares to make a quilt, see page 7 for quilt instructions. If you are not making a quilt, follow instructions below to make hot pads from individual squares. The hot pad is a two-day project—30 minutes each day.

Materials: Muslin, paraffin, double boiler, coffee cans, large stainless steel pot, stove or hot plate, measuring cup, strainer, large stiff-bristle paintbrushes or sponges, scissors, measuring tape, paper towels, newspapers, iron, alum, cream of tartar, nature items for making natural dyes.

(Natural dyes can be made from almost any natural material—berries, leaves, pods, fruit and skins, flowers, weeds, nuts, etc. You will want to experiment. You will need about one pound of dye material per three to four yards of fabric.)

To make hot pad—fiberfill batting, straight pins, quilting thread, seam binding, additional muslin. For each student—one quilting needle.

Preparation: Wash and dry muslin to preshrink. Cut muslin into 9-inch (22.5-cm) squares—one for each student. To make hot pads, cut additional muslin squares—one for each student. Cut batting into 9-inch (22.5-cm) squares—one for each student. Also cut seam binding into 40-inch (100-cm) lengths—one for each student.

Fill pot with dye material and cover with water. Boil for about an hour (less for berries and plants, more for nut shells and stems) and strain. Cool.

Dissolve 3 oz. alum and 1/2 oz. cream of tartar in 1 cup water. This solution is called mordant. (Mordant prepares cloth so the dye will bite into fabric.)

Add mordant to the dye, then add water to dilute the dye concentrate. (The more concentrated your dye, the darker your fabric will be.)

Place paraffin in coffee can. Place coffee can in double boiler and heat.

Instruct each student in the following procedures:
- Place muslin square on pad of newspapers. Paint wax design on fabric, using brush or dabbing with sponge (sketch a). Wax should penetrate cloth and look transparent in order to resist dye. Let cool.
- When wax has cooled, crumple up fabric square, then smooth out and place in cool dye bath.
- When fabric has reached desired shade, remove from dye and place on pad of newspapers. Cover with paper towels and a layer of newspaper, then iron at high setting until all wax has melted out of fabric (sketch b). Let square dry.

If you are making a quilt, see page 7. If students are making hot pads, they follow these procedures:
- Place batik square facedown. Place a layer of batting and then the plain muslin square on top of the batik square. Secure with straight pins (sketch c).
- Pin seam binding around edges of square (sketch d). Stitch.
- Optional: Stitch around design as shown in sketch e.

Pioneer Life: **Pioneers lived in a time and place when the land was just about the way God had created it. There was beauty and color all around. The spring was especially beautiful because of the many wildflowers that sprang up on the hillsides. These wildflowers and other natural items were sometimes used to make dyes for cosmetics, clothing and basketry.**

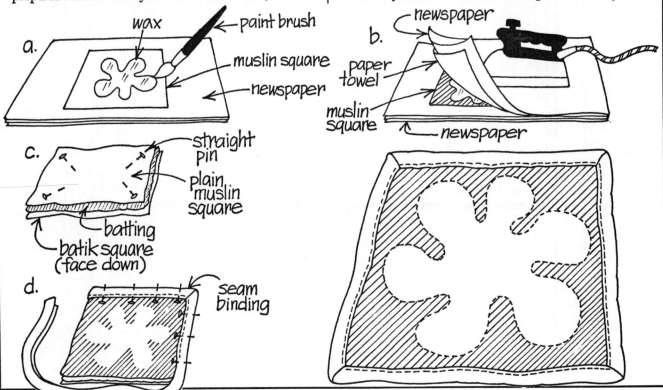

a. wax — paint brush — muslin square — newspaper

b. newspaper — paper towel — muslin square — newspaper

c. straight pin — plain muslin square — batting — batik square (face down)

d. seam binding

CANDLE SHELLS
(ONE-DAY PROJECT / 30 MINUTES)

Materials: Paraffin, crayons or candle dye, double boiler, coffee cans, stove or hot plate, candy thermometer, sharp knives, several awls or skewers, several candles, matches. For each student—food-warming candle, several small, round balloons.

Instruct each student in the following procedures:

- Place paraffin in coffee can. Place coffee can in double boiler and heat paraffin to 160 degrees F. Add crayons to melted wax.
- Stretch mouth of balloon around water faucet and hold firmly as you partially fill balloon with tepid water. Remove balloon from faucet and tie.
- Dip balloon into hot wax as many times as needed to form a 1/4-inch (.6-cm) "shell" around bottom half of balloon (sketch a).
- As soon as shell has cooled enough to handle, pop balloon, pour out water and remove from shell.
- Trim edge of shell with knife while wax is still warm (sketch b). Be careful not to press too hard.
- Heat knife, awls or skewers over candle flame and use to carve designs into warm wax on top one-third of shell (sketch c).
- Place food-warming candle in shell. Candle shell may be floated on water (sketch d).

Pioneer Life: **How do you know when it's time for you to get up in the morning? When do you usually go to bed? The pioneers' day often revolved around the time the sun rose and set. They would usually get up at sun-up and go to bed when the sun went down. Since there was no electricity, if pioneers needed to stay up after dark, they had to build a fire or use candles to provide light.**

BEADED KEY CHAIN
(ONE-DAY PROJECT / 30 MINUTES)

Materials: Scissors, 1/8-inch (.3-cm) suede strips. For each student—one metal 1½-inch (3.75-cm) split key ring, 29 6×9-mm pony beads (including seven beads of a contrasting color).

Preparation: Cut suede into 16-inch (40-cm) lengths—three for each student. Trim ends of suede on a slant.

Instruct each student in the following procedures:

- Knot each length of suede around ring (sketch a).
- Thread strips c and d through first bead (sketch b). Bead will be tight—use a rotating motion to "screw" bead onto strips. Slide bead to knot.
- Thread strips *b* and *c* through one bead. Then thread strips *d* and *e* through one bead (sketch b).
- Thread strips *c* and *d* through a bead of contrasting color (sketch c).
- Thread two beads on strips *a* and *b*, then thread two more on strips *e* and *f* (sketch c).
- Thread beads on *b* and *c*, *d* and *e*, and *c* and *d* (sketch d).
- On the end of each strip, thread three beads, including one of contrasting color. Knot ends of strips (sketch d).

Pioneer Life: **What type of clothing is a status symbol among your friends? The Indians in pioneer times had a code of fashion, too. They often made beautiful clothes from the skins of animals and decorated them with colorful beadwork. Sometimes the chief of a tribe would wear an elaborate headdress made from leather, bird feathers and colored beads. If a man wore this headdress, everyone who saw him knew he held an important position in the tribe.**

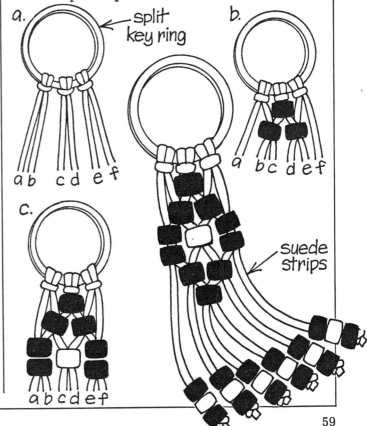

CORNHUSK DOLLS
(ONE- OR TWO-DAY PROJECT / 60 MINUTES)

Materials: Dried cornhusks (available at craft supply stores), dishpan, warm water, newspapers, scissors, heavy string, chenille wires, straight pins, glue, Styrofoam cups.

Preparation: Soak cornhusks in warm water for 5-10 minutes, then drain on newspapers. Husks should be wet while students work.

Instruct each student in the following procedures:

- To make doll's head: Use string to tie ends of four to five husks together (sketch a). (Note: Always wrap string around husks more than once before tying knot so husks will not fall apart.) Wrap several narrow strips of husk around tied ends to form head (sketch b). Turn doll upside down and fold long husks down over head. Tie with string (sketch c). Then tie a narrow strip of cornhusk around neck.
- To make arms: Wrap one chenille wire lengthwise with a strip of husk. Tie ends with string, then tie a narrow strip of cornhusk over each string (sketch d).
- To make woman's sleeves: Tie one husk around end of arm (sketch e). Fold sleeve back over arm and tie (sketch f). Repeat on other end of chenille wire to make other sleeve.
- To make body: Place arm piece between layers of husk below doll's head (sketch g). Roll narrow strips of husk into a cylinder. Place ball between layers of husk, below arms, to form chest. Tie below chest (sketch h). Drape a wide husk strip over each shoulder, crossing strips in front and back. Tie string around waist to secure in place (sketch i).
- To make woman's skirt: With pointed ends at waist and wide ends over the head, place several wide husks around doll's body (sketch j). Tie securely with string. Fold down skirt and trim ends (sketch k). Pin skirt husks together (if necessary) for drying. Place doll on inverted Styrofoam cup and dry overnight. Remove the pins and glue the skirt husks together as necessary.
- For man doll: Make head, arms and body as described above. Bend chenille wire for legs and feet (sketch l). Place wire between husks below waist. Divide "body" husks into two sections and tie at the bottom of each leg. Wrap narrow strips around uncovered wire at feet and ankles (sketch m). Tie a narrow strip of husk around man's waist.

Enrichment Idea: Add corn silk for hair. Use additional husk strips to make bonnets, hats and other accessories.

Pioneer Life: Many pioneers settled on the prairie and became farmers. One of the most common crops grown was corn because it was so hardy. Pioneer farmers sold the corn to make money and they sometimes used the husks of the corn to make things like dolls, mats or trivets. (See Braided Cornhusk Mat, page 62.)

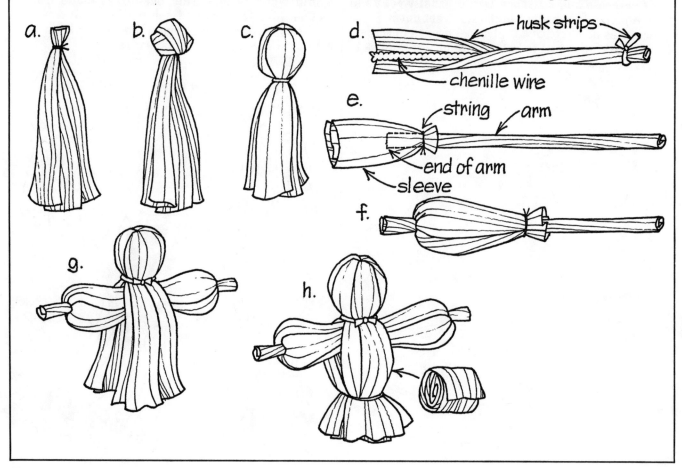

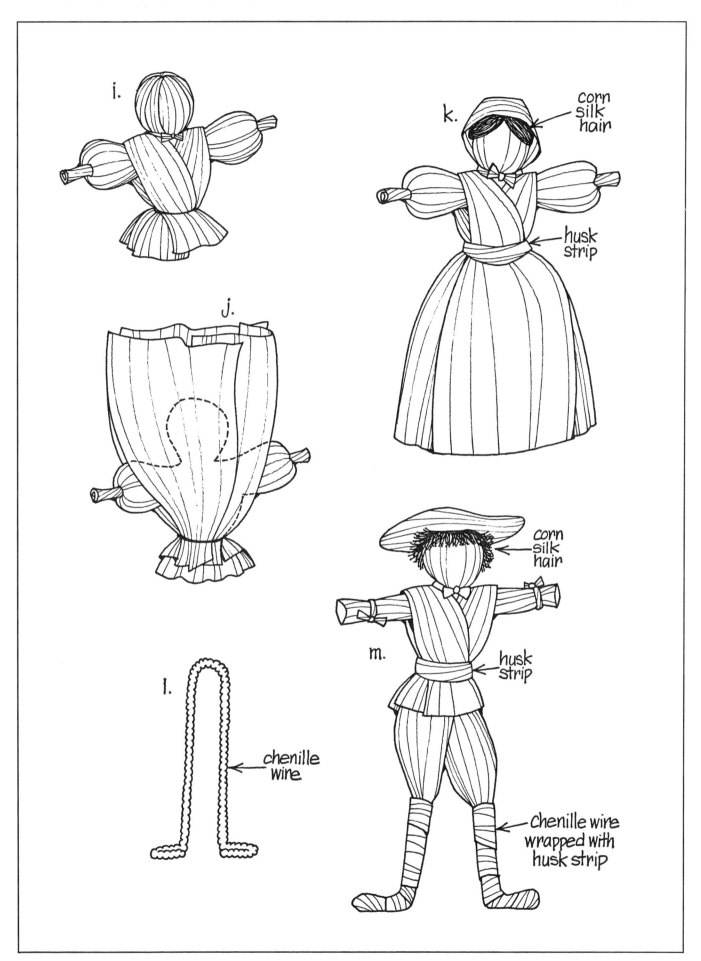

i.

k.

corn
silk
hair

husk
strip

j.

l.

chenille
wire

m.

corn
silk
hair

husk
strip

chenille wire
wrapped with
husk strip

BRAIDED CORNHUSK MAT
(ONE- OR TWO-DAY PROJECT / 60 MINUTES)

Materials: Cornhusks (available at craft supply stores), heavy-duty thread, scissors, ruler, dishpan, warm water, old towels, thumbtacks, straight pins. For each student—one small board, one large needle.

Preparation: Soak husks in warm water for about five minutes. (Husks should be kept damp as students work.)

Instruct each student in the following procedures:
- Tear damp husks lengthwise into strips about 1 inch (2.5-cm) wide.
- Tie ends of three strips together with thread.
- Use thumbtack to attach the three strips to board. Braid the husks (sketch a). To add new strips: Fold strip lengthwise as you braid and push a small section of a new strip into the folded section (sketch b). (Do not add three new strips at one time. The braid will be weak and pull apart.) Continue adding strips and braiding until your braid is about 9 feet long. Tie end with thread. (To finish this craft in one hour students should braid for no longer than 30 minutes. If the braid is not 9 feet long a smaller mat may still be completed.)
- Begin shaping mat by coiling braid, either flat-sided or on edge.
- Experiment with design to make interesting patterns. Students may choose to make a round, oval or square mat. Use thumbtacks or straight pins to fasten coil to the board in several places to hold shape.
- Keeping mat pinned to board, begin at center of spiral and sew adjacent strands of braid together with zigzag stitches (sketch c). Work from the center to the outside edge of mat.
- Allow mat to dry flat overnight.

Pioneer Life: (See Cornhusk Dolls, page 60.)

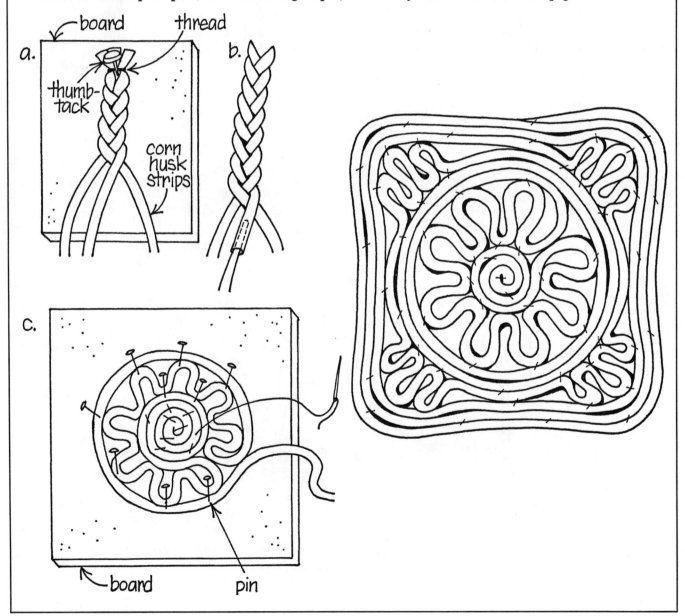

FOX AND GEESE GAME

(ONE- OR TWO-DAY PROJECT / 60 MINUTES)

Materials: Acrylic paints and paintbrushes, clear acrylic spray, rulers, pencils, felt, yarn, scissors, plate or bowl 8 inches (20-cm) in diameter, newspapers, photocopier, 3/4-inch (1.9-cm) pressboard, saw. For each student—26 corn kernels or pebbles.

Preparation: Photocopy game board and instructions—one copy for each student. Use saw to cut pressboard into 8-inch (20-cm) squares—one for each student. Cut yarn into 20-inch (50-cm) lengths—one for each student. Cover work area with newspaper.

Instruct each student in the following procedures:

FOR GAME BOARD AND PLAYING PIECES:

- Using a pencil and ruler, draw game board diagram on wood square.
- Carefully paint the penciled diagram on game board, filling in circles. (You may want to use one color for the lines and another color for the circles.)
- Optional: Draw and paint a border or additional decoration on pressboard, outside of game diagram.
- Paint 24 corn kernels (or pebbles) yellow for geese; paint 2 kernels red for foxes.
- Spray dry kernels and game board with clear acrylic spray.

FOR POUCH:

- Place bowl or plate on felt. Trace around perimeter and cut out circle.
- Using scissors, cut slits at 1/2-inch (1.25-cm) intervals around edge of felt circle (sketch a).

- Thread a length of yarn through slits. Pull drawstring tight and tie a bow to make pouch for corn kernels (sketch b)
- Play game.

Pioneer Life: **Pioneer children and youth didn't have a lot of free time for recreation. Often they helped their parents build log cabins, plant crops and take care of animals. When there was a spare moment, young pioneers enjoyed playing home-made games such as Fox and Geese.**

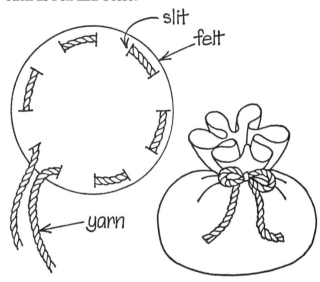

FOX AND GEESE GAME BOARD AND INSTRUCTIONS

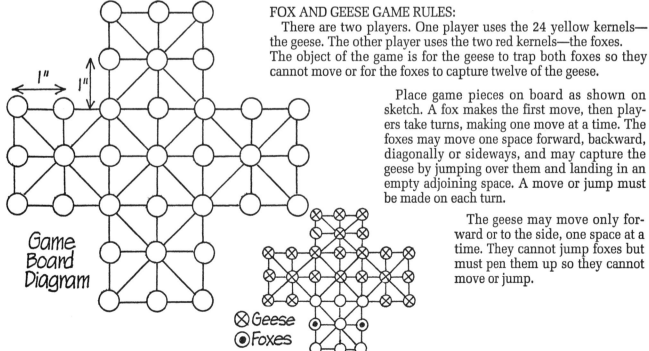

Game Board Diagram

⊗ Geese
⊙ Foxes

FOX AND GEESE GAME RULES:

There are two players. One player uses the 24 yellow kernels—the geese. The other player uses the two red kernels—the foxes. The object of the game is for the geese to trap both foxes so they cannot move or for the foxes to capture twelve of the geese.

Place game pieces on board as shown on sketch. A fox makes the first move, then players take turns, making one move at a time. The foxes may move one space forward, backward, diagonally or sideways, and may capture the geese by jumping over them and landing in an empty adjoining space. A move or jump must be made on each turn.

The geese may move only forward or to the side, one space at a time. They cannot jump foxes but must pen them up so they cannot move or jump.

PAPER MAKING

(ONE-DAY PROJECT / 60 MINUTES)

Materials: Saw, hammer, nails, 1-inch (2.5-cm) plywood, old window screen, staple gun, staples, scissors, sponges, iron, blender, measuring cup, large spoon, dishpan, warm water, newspapers, any combination of the following: paper bags, paper napkins, paper towels, newspapers, cornhusks, sawdust, dry leaves, dry grass, dry onion skins or dry fruit skins.

Preparation: To make paper mold: Cut eight 1×6-inch (2.5×15-cm) strips of wood. Nail wood strips together to make two frames. Trace around one of the frames onto screen and cut on traced lines. On one frame, staple screen (sketch a). Make one two-part mold for every three students. Fill dishpan with warm water. Cover work area with newspaper.

Instruct each student in the following procedures:

• Cut or tear all vegetable fibers and paper into small pieces and soak in warm water until saturated. The resulting pulp mixture is called slurry.

• Scoop out about one cup of slurry, put in blender and add water to fill blender. Blend for a few seconds.

• Place the two parts of mold together, with the screen on the bottom frame facing up (sketch b). Hold mold over the dishpan and pour slurry over mold. Allow water to drain into dishpan (sketch c). The mash left on the screen is called wet leaf.

• Remove top frame carefully. Place several thicknesses of newspaper on top of wet leaf.

• Turn frame and newspaper facedown on table. Use sponge to dab away excess water through screen (sketch d).

• Carefully remove screen (sketch e).

• Place several thicknesses of newspaper on top of wet leaf and iron dry (sketch f). If necessary, change newspapers once or twice. Remove newspapers. You will have a coarse, thick sheet of paper.

Pioneer Life: **Most pioneers didn't make their own paper. By that time paper was being made from wood pulp in paper mills. Still, pioneers didn't have a lot of paper, so they probably used what they had carefully. Many pioneers carried notebooks with them as they traveled west. In these journals, they recorded details about their lives. Today, we can read copies of these journals to find out what pioneer life was like.**

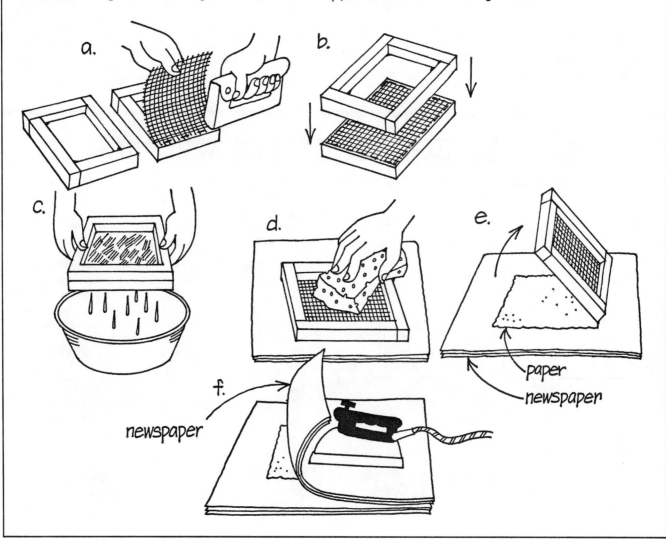

a.

b.

c.

d.

e.

paper
newspaper

f.

newspaper

CLIMBING PULL TOY
(TWO-DAY PROJECT / 60 MINUTES)

Materials: Flour, cornstarch, salt, glycerin (available in pharmacies or drug stores), large mixing bowls, cookie sheets, toothpicks, table knives, rolling pin, large spoon, measuring cups and measuring spoons, plastic bag, oven, acrylic paints, paintbrushes, measuring sticks, aluminum foil, yarn or heavy string, 1-inch (2.5-cm) plywood, saw, electric drill with a 1/2-inch (.3-cm) drill bit, clear acrylic spray, scissors, water. For each student—two pony beads or buttons.

Preparation: Make dough using the following recipe: Mix 1 cup water with 2 tsp. glycerin. In a separate bowl, mix 2 cups flour, 1 cup cornstarch, 1 cup salt. Combine wet and dry ingredients. Knead for 5 minutes until smooth. Recipe makes enough for six students. Store dough in plastic bag. Cut wood into 1×6-inch (2.5×15-cm) pieces—one for each student. Drill three holes in each piece of wood (sketch a).

Instruct each student in the following procedures:
DAY ONE:
- Use rolling pin to flatten dough to 1/4-inch (.6-cm) thickness.
- Use toothpick to draw a figure about 6 inches (15-cm) tall, with outstretched arms measuring about 4 inches (10-cm) from hand to hand. Cut out figure with table knife. Place figure on cookie sheet.

- Wrap foil around two toothpicks and insert vertically through figure's hands (sketch b).
- Bake figure in oven set at 450 degrees for 10-15 minutes. Remove and let cool.
DAY TWO:
- Remove toothpicks.
- Paint character and let dry, then spray with clear acrylic spray.
- Cut two pieces of yarn or string about 3 feet (90 cm) long. Cut one piece of yarn 6 inches (15-cm) long.
- Thread longer strings through holes on ends of wooden bar and knot on top.
- Thread the same strings through hands of figure. Tie a bead or button at end of each string (sketch c).
- Fold shorter length of string in half, thread through center hole in bar and knot for hanger.
- Hang bar from any available hook. Pull strings, alternating left and right. Figure will climb up strings. Relax tension to see figure slide down.

Pioneer Life: **Christmas and birthday celebrations were much simpler during pioneer days. Family members didn't exchange lots of expensive gifts. Most gifts were home-made. A pioneer child might have been delighted to receive a hand-made toy such as the Climbing Pull Toy.**

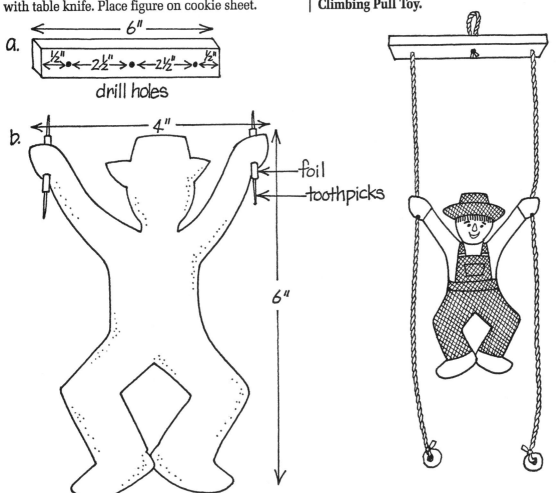

a. 6"

1/2" 2½" 2½" 1/2"

drill holes

b. 4"

foil
toothpicks

6"

PUNCHED TIN ORNAMENTS
(ONE- OR TWO-DAY PROJECT / 60 MINUTES)

Materials: Tin snips and/or sturdy scissors, nails in various sizes (sharp chisels and awls are also nice for variety), hammers, pliers, grease pencils, rags, newspapers, wood scraps, enamel paints (transparent spray colors are especially nice for this project), paintbrushes, paint thinner, coffee can for cleaning brushes, string or fishing line. For each student—a few tin can lids in a variety of sizes, one or more clear plastic suction cups.

Instruct each student in the following procedures:
• Use grease pencil to draw a design on lid.
• Use one or both of the following techniques to decorate ornament:
   1. Use tin snips or scissors to cut and pliers to bend lid into desired shape. (Suggest students practice on extra lids to see if their designs are workable.)
   2. Place several thicknesses of newspaper over wood. Place tin lid on pad. Use hammer and nail, awl or chisel to punch design.
• Pound a hole at top center of ornament for hanging.
• Paint ornaments. (A coat of fast-drying spray paint followed by brushed-on details works well.) Let dry.
• Use paint thinner to clean paintbrushes.
• Thread string or fishing line through top center hole and knot for hanger.
• Attach string to suction cup and hang in a window.

Pioneer Life: Lanterns, pans, cups and pots made out of tin were common and much-used items among pioneers. Today we often throw tin cans away. Can you think of ways to reuse tin cans instead of throwing them away?

WOODEN BOOK SHELF
(ONE- OR TWO-DAY PROJECT / 60 MINUTES)

Materials: Hammers, 1-inch brads (nails), sandpaper, wood glue, wet rag, pencils, ruler or measuring tape, coping or hacksaw, acrylic paints, paintbrushes, clear acrylic spray, 3/4-inch (1.8-cm) pine board, 3/8×1/2-inch (.9×17.5-cm) round edge stop (available at lumber supply stores).

Preparation: Cut pine into 4½×7-inch (11.25×17.5-cm) pieces—two for each student. Cut additional wood into 4½×12-inch (11.25×30-cm) pieces—two for each student. Cut edge stop into 3½-inch (8.75-cm) lengths—four for each student.

Instruct each student in the following procedures:
• Use sandpaper to sand rough edges of all pieces.
• Nail trough pieces together at a right angle (sketch a).
• Place trough against one end piece and use pencil to lightly mark position of trough as in sketch b. (Note that back piece of trough is higher than front piece.) Mark second end piece. (The pencil marks will help you keep trough aligned when nailing it to end boards.)
• Glue and nail edge stop pieces to bottom edges of trough as in sketch c.
• Place trough against end piece along pencil lines. Attach end piece by nailing edge stops to it (sketch d).
• Repeat previous step to attach other end piece to bookshelf.
• Paint design on shelf ends. Let dry and spray with clear acrylic spray.

Enrichment Idea: Make stencils using patterns on page 10. Students paint stencil designs on ends of book shelf.

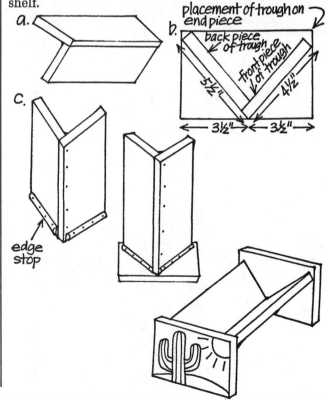

SECTION 5
REPRODUCIBLE PAGES

BIBLE MEMORY VERSE COLORING PAGES

The following pages are reproducible and contain ten Bible Memory Verse designs for younger elementary children and ten for older elementary children. Ideas for using these pages include:

1. Use the photocopied pages as rewards for children who memorize the Bible verse. They may take the page home to color and display.

2. Use the pages in class for transition times or for advanced students who finish an activity ahead of other students.

3. Play a coloring game. Place a variety of felt pens on the table. Recite the verse together. Then each student may choose a pen and use it to color on his or her page for one minute. When time is up, students put pens down and repeat verse together again. Students then choose another pen and color for one minute. Repeat process until pages are completed or students tire of activity.

4. To customize pages, cover the Bible verse with white paper and letter another verse or saying in its place before you photocopy.

STUDENT CERTIFICATES AND AWARDS

The awards and certificates on the following pages may be personalized for various uses. Just follow these simple procedures:

1. Tear out certificate and letter the name of your program on the appropriate line.

2. Photocopy as many copies of certificate as needed.

3. Letter each child's certificate with his or her name (and achievement when appropriate).

" I am with you always, to the very end of the age. " Matthew 28:20

"Everyone who believes in him receives forgiveness of sins through his name." Acts 10:43

"Command them to do good, to be rich in good deeds, and to be generous and willing to share." 1 Timothy 6:18

"If you love me, you will obey what I command." John 14:15

"Encourage one another and build each other up, just as in fact you are doing." 1 Thessalonians 5:11

"Accept one another, then, just as Christ accepted you, in order to bring praise to God."
Romans 15:7

"Share with God's people who are in need." Romans 12:13

"Go into all the world and preach the good news to all creation." Mark 16:15

"God...wants all men to be SAVED and to come to a knowledge of the TRUTH."

1 Timothy 2:4

"Boldly and without hindrance he preached the kingdom of God and taught about the Lord Jesus Christ." Acts 28:31

"I am with you always, to the very end of the age." Matthew 28:20

"Everyone who believes in him receives forgiveness of sins through his name." Acts 10:43

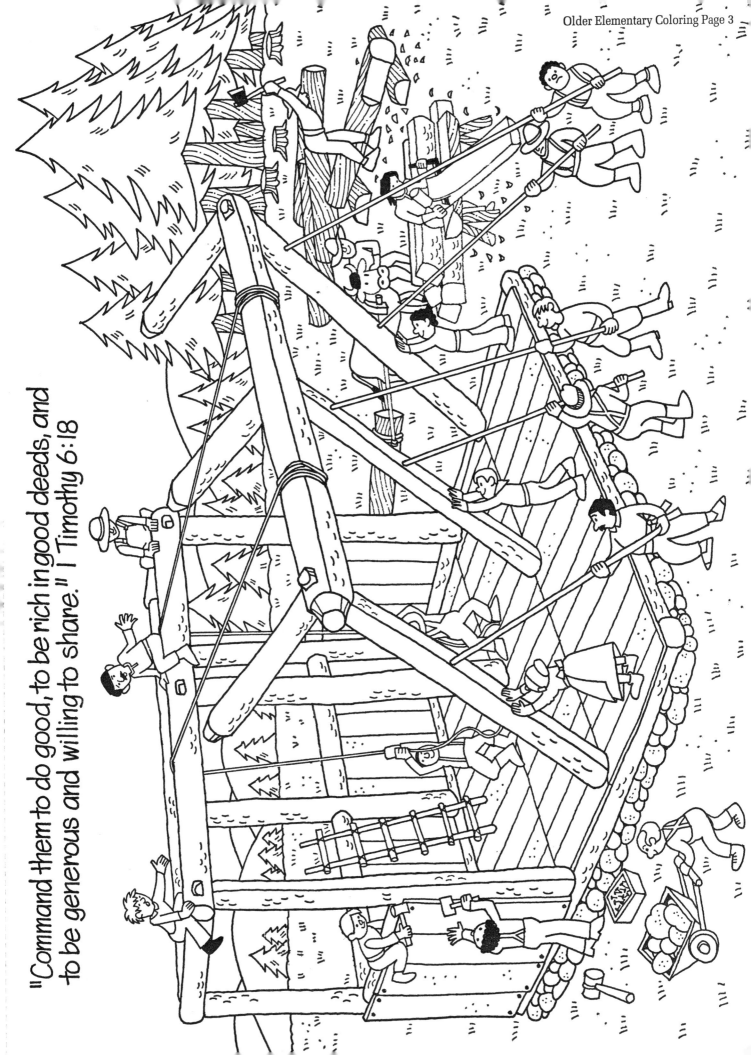

"Command them to do good, to be rich in good deeds, and to be generous and willing to share." I Timothy 6:18

"If you love me, you will obey what I command." John 14:15

"Encourage one another and build each other up, just as in fact you are doing." 1 Thessalonians 5:11

"Accept one another, then, just as Christ accepted you, in order to bring praise to God." Romans 15:7

"Share with God's people who are in need."

Romans 12:13

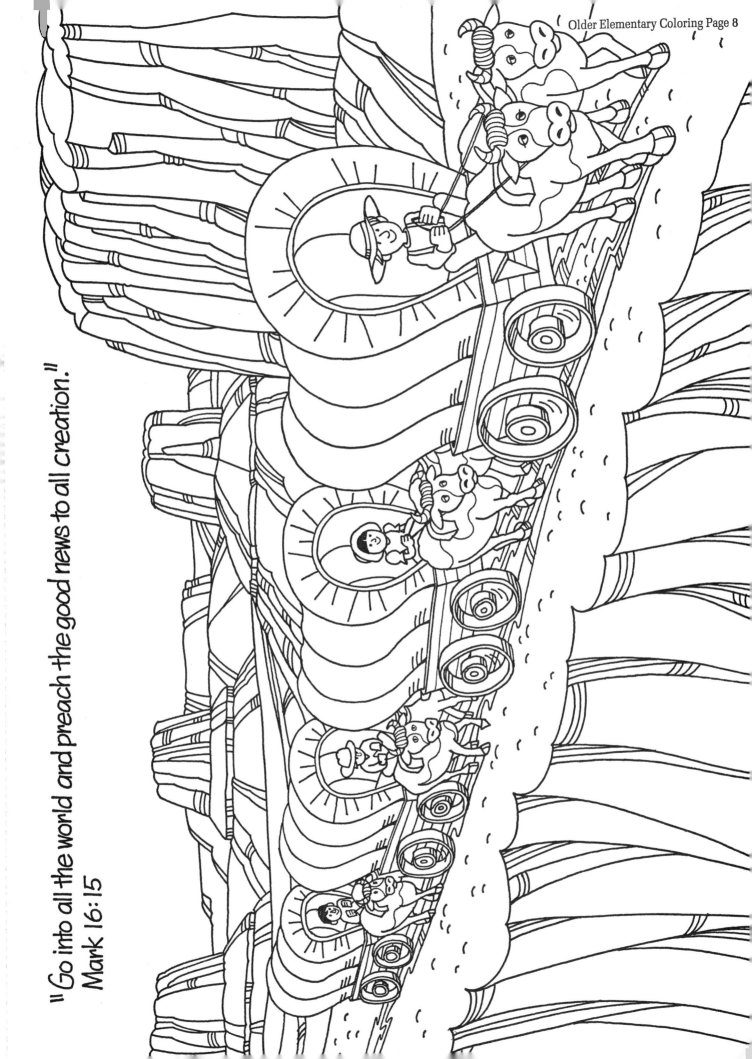

"Go into all the world and preach the good news to all creation."
Mark 16:15

"God...wants all men to be saved and to come to a knowledge of the truth."
I Timothy 2:4

"Boldly and without hindrance he preached the kingdom of God and taught about the Lord Jesus Christ." Acts 28:31

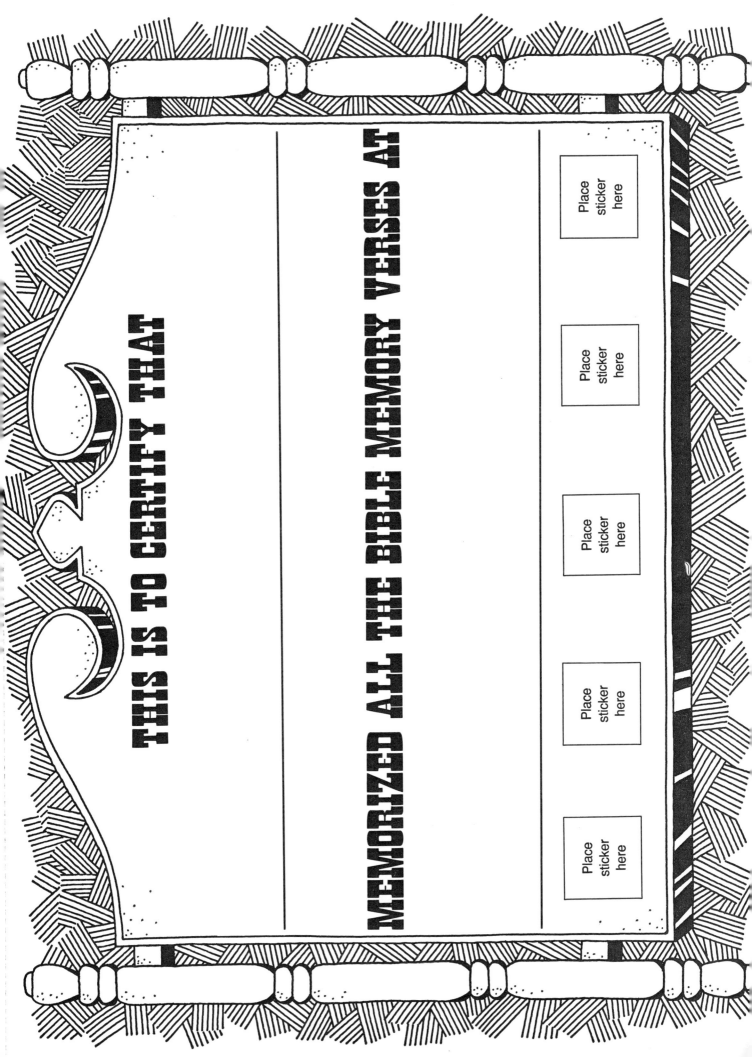

THIS IS TO CERTIFY THAT

MEMORIZED ALL THE BIBLE MEMORY VERSES AT

Place sticker here

Place sticker here

Place sticker here

Place sticker here

Place sticker here

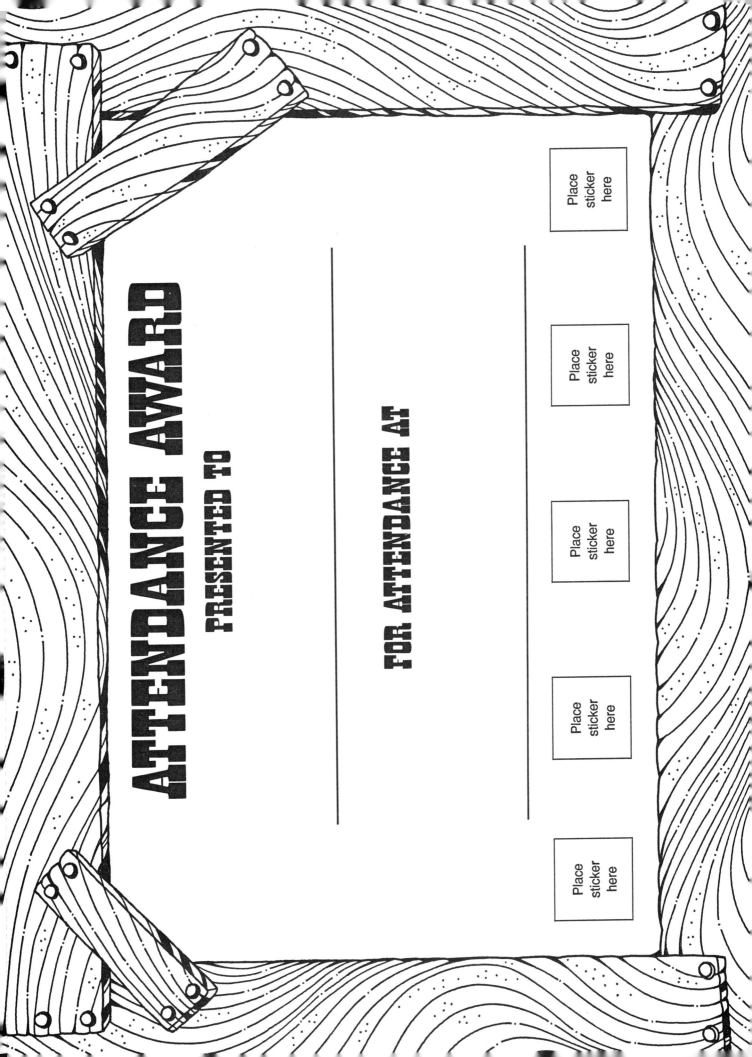

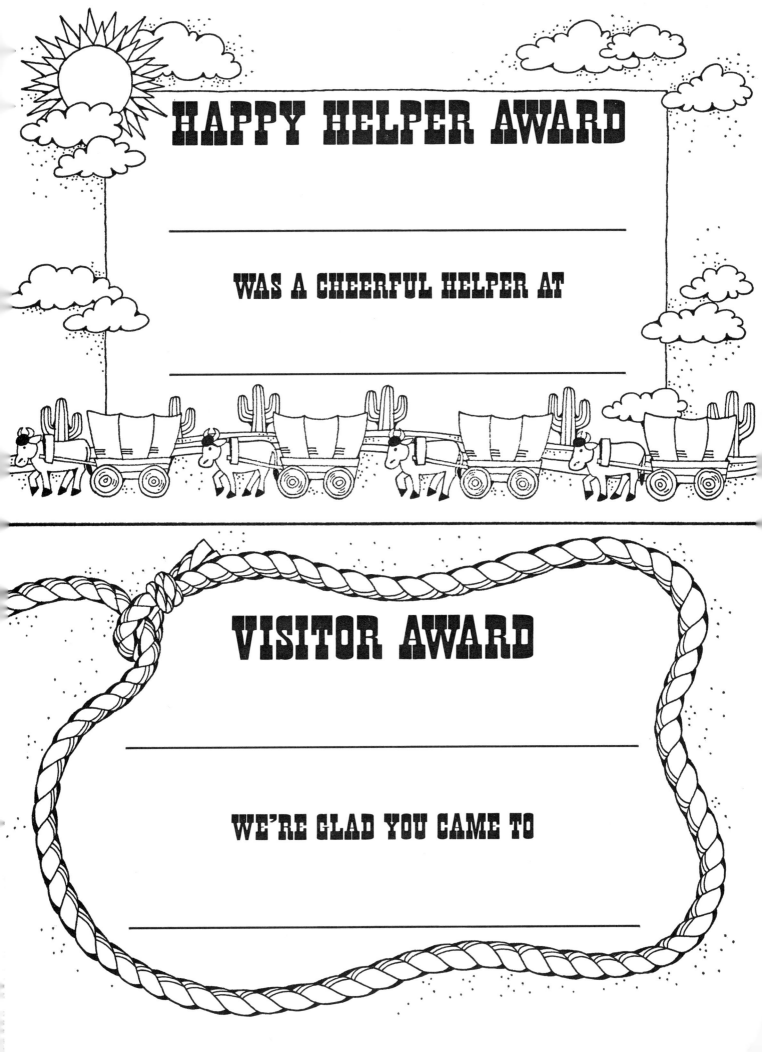

HAPPY HELPER AWARD

_____

WAS A CHEERFUL HELPER AT

_____

VISITOR AWARD

_____

WE'RE GLAD YOU CAME TO

_____

SHARING AWARD

_____

SHARED _____ **WITH** _____

"Command them to do good, to be rich in good deeds,
and to be generous and willing to share."
1 Timothy 6:18

THANKS A HEAP FOR

_____

_____

Sticker Poster

INDEX